Japanese Flower Arrangement
IKEBANA
STEP-BY-STEP

DISTRIBUTORS:
UNITED STATES: Kodansha America, Inc., through Farrar, Straus & Giroux, 19 Union Square West, New York, NY 10003.
CANADA: Fitzhenry & Whiteside Ltd., 195 Allstate Parkway, Markham, Ontario L3R 4T8.
BRITISH ISLES AND EUROPEAN CONTINENT: Premier Book Marketing Ltd., 1 Gower Street, London WC1E 6HA.
AUSTRALIA AND NEW ZEALAND: Bookwise International, 54 Crittenden Road, Findon, South Australia 5023.
JAPAN: Japan Publications Trading Co., Ltd., 1-2-1, Sarugaku-cho, Chiyoda-ku, Tokyo, 101 Japan.

First edition 1995, 4th printing May 1998
Original Copyright © 1995 by Reiko Takenaka
World rights reserved by JOIE, INC. 1-8-3, Hirakawa-cho, Chiyoda-ku, Tokyo 102 Japan;
Printed in China.

ISBN0-87040-958-1

ACKNOWLEDGMENTS

My grateful appreciation to the following individuals for their encouragement and patience throughout the many months it took to compile this book.

Shiro Shimura, publisher, JOIE, INC.
Yasunori Komatsu, Yasuaki Okada, Yoshiki Nakano, photographers
Yoko Ishiguro, translator
Miyoko Tachibana, illustrator
Akira Naito, chief-editor
Mitsue Hashimoto, Mieko Baba, editors

Reiko Takenaka

FOREWORD

Ikebana is hospitality from the heart, using various plant materials. It is an art in which the force of life expressed in living plants and the spirit of the person arranging them speak deeply to each other and unite to create new beauty and form. By devoting one's heart to flowers, one can in an informal, natural way provide pleasure for family and guests and together spend many a refreshing hour! Ikebana brings a richness to our lives!

I produced this book to acquaint as many people as possible with the joy and delight of Ikebana. I have avoided strict rules of traditional arrangement in order to give my heart free reign in creating Ikebana which is suitable to the space it occupies. For vases I have used common household articles, showing how new beauty can be created with originality when using only a small amount of floral material. Here indeed is the charm of Ikebana!

I have explained how to arrange flowers so that anyone with a little skill and sensitivity can do Ikebana. I will be grateful if this book can bring pleasure to you.

What makes Ikebana fresh is the enlivened sensitivity of those who do Ikebana. Giving thanks for the bounties of nature, I hope to continue expanding my activities, using Ikebana as a living, creative entity in space.

Flowers convey a heartwarming message which crosses the barriers of nationality and language. I would like to express my heartfelt thanks to the JOIE, INC., publishers of this book, for having helped me to meet so many people through Ikebana.

July 1995
Tokyo,

Reiko Takenaka

CONTENTS

MOOD-CREATING IDEAS

◆WINDOWSILL

Put cheerful flowers or a romantic bloom on a sunny windowsill, arranged freely to your taste.

1 Spacing and clarity of the various glasses create a rhythm for the eyes to follow although the arrangement is not uniform. Various colors add interest.

Materials: Clematis, Thalictrum, Cockscomb, Maidenhair fern, Caladium, Asparagus fern, Prairie gentian
Containers: 3 stemmed glasses, tumbler, short and wide jar
Finished size: W 114 cm × H 37 cm (44½″ × 14½″)
●**Tips:** Every flower has its own features. Try to show the best figure of each, and finish with asparagus fern.

Most people think ikebana needs special vases and utensils. But it's not true. Feel free to use your imagination and enjoy different ways of using everyday utensils.

Freestyle arrangements using multi-containers.

Try various layouts.

2

Make the mood casual as if the wind is blowing through the flowers.

Materials: Cape marigold, Spirea
Containers: 3 tumblers
Finished size: W 61 cm × H 31 cm
(23¾" × 12")

●**Tips:**
Arrange spirea with a movement, while setting cape marigold altering each height and direction.

3

Two desert candles leaning toward each other. The fullness of the myriocladus anchors the long-stemmed desert candles.

Materials: Desert candle, Myriocladus
Containers: 2 tumblers
Finished size: W 64 cm × H 60 cm
(25" × 23½")

See page 76 for arranging steps.

◆WINDOWSILL

4 Soaring height of the calla lilies draws one's attention to the rich spaciousness around the arrangement.

Materials: Calla lily, Lobster claw, Stenophyllum
Container: Decorative plant pot
Others: *Kenzan* (needlepoint holder), Small vessel
Finished size: W 38 cm × H 81 cm (14¾″ × 31½″)

See page 77 for arranging steps.

5

As in this case, the characteristics of the accompanying flowers can change the mood of the ornamental, by creating contrast.

Materials: Alocasia, Baby's breath, Statice
Container: Flowerpot
Finished size: W 52 cm × H 50 cm
(20¼″ × 19½″)
See page 77 for arranging steps.

6

A lone safflower creates an elegant focal point at the crossing of the stems of the impactful window plant.

Materials: Window plant, Safflower, Solidaster
Container: Modern-designed drinking glass
Finished size: W 53 cm × H 23 cm
(20½″ × 9″)

Materials:
Window plant (**A**), Safflower (**B**), Solidaster (**C**)

A

B

C

38 cm
(14¾″)

●**Quick Steps:**

1. Resting stem ends at inside of container, lean each stem left and right.

2. Stand safflower upright in middle, and add solidaster to hide stems.

◆ WINDOWSILL

7

The contrast of red and green and the curvy lines of gerbera daisies stress the beauty and the delicacy of this arrangement.

Materials: Gerbera daisy, Japanese bead, Delta maidenhair fern
Container: Irregular-shaped vase
Finished size: W 52 cm × H 63 cm
(20¼″ × 24½″)

See page **78** for arranging steps.

8

Like the golden sunshine on a field, the patrinia scabiosafolias enhance the yellow of the sunflowers.

Materials: Sunflower, Patrinia scabiosafolia
Container: Tube-shaped vase
Finished size: W 31 cm × H 41 cm
(12″ × 16″)

See page **79** for arranging steps.

9

Make a fashionable arrangement by contrasting the strong lines of anthurium with the delicate airiness of asparagus fern, grounded by pastel roses.

Materials: Anthurium leaf, Asparagus fern, Rose
Container: Cookie jar
Others: *Kenzan* (needlepoint holder)
Finished size: W 71 cm × H 42 cm
(27¾″ × 16¼″)
See page 80 for arranging steps.

10

The orange kaffir lilies focus the multi-directional leaves of hosta.

Materials: Hosta, Kaffir lily
Container: Color-blocked planter
Others: *Kenzan* (needlepoint holder), *Kansui-seki* (white Japanese marble)
Finished size: W 56 cm × H 37 cm
(21¾″ × 14½″)
See page 81 for arranging steps.

◆ BEDROOMS

You don't have to spend a lot on flowers. Sometimes, your favorite flowers picked from your own garden and arranged in a favorite household container give the warmest feelings, with their natural lines.

11 The tendrils of ivy flow from the container as if it had grown there, giving the whole arrangement a natural feeling.

Materials: Ivy, Croton, Orange flare cosmos
Container: Beer mug
Finished size: W 53 cm × H 28 cm (20½″ × 11″)

See page 76 for arranging steps.

Charming decorations using favorite everyday cups and bottles.

12

Your favorite mug can be a nice holder for a casual arrangement of seasonal flowers.

Materials: Cornflower, Gerbera daisy, Miniature rose
Container: Coffee mug
Others: *Kenzan* (needlepoint holder)
Finished size: W 43 cm × H 33 cm
(16¾″ × 12¾″)

See page 82 for arranging steps.

13

Make the best use of matching containers by varying the heights of the flowers.

Materials: Gerbera daisy, Begonia
Containers: 2 hot whiskey glasses
Finished size: W 24 cm × H 38 cm
(9¼″ × 14¾″)

●**Tips:**
Rest begonia against rim of glass, and stand gerbera upright with flower facing up.

14

The clear glass bottle and the lacy leaves of caladium create a refreshing atmosphere.

Materials: Caladium, Rose, Ageratum
Container: Decorative glass bottle
Finished size: W 44 cm × H 59 cm (17¼″ × 23″)

See page 80 for arranging steps.

13

◈ BEDROOMS

15

The reflection of the glorious peonies doubles the effect.

Materials: Peony, Palm, Dracaena
Container: Planter
Others: *Kenzan* (needlepoint holder)
Finished size: W 53 cm × H 58 cm
    (20½″ × 22½″)
See page 83 for arranging steps.

16

Accentuate one distinctive shape with another for an elegant touch.

Materials: Blue fantasy, Glory lily
Container: Perfume bottle
Finished size: W 34 cm × H 35 cm
    (13½″ × 13¾″)

Materials: Blue fantasy (**A**), Glory lily (**B**)

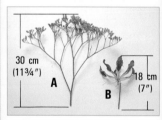

30 cm
(11¾″) **A**
    B 18 cm (7″)

● **Quick Steps:**

1. Stand blue fantasy vertically to take advantage of its width.

2. Slip stem of glory lily behind blue fantasy so that flower faces you.

17

The dainty perfume bottle holds the slender stems of this bold arrangement.

Materials: Begonia, Alocasia
Container: Perfume bottle
Finished size: W 36 cm × H 46 cm
(14″ × 18″)

Materials: Begonia (**A**), Alocasia (**B**)

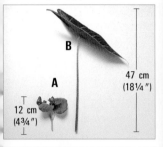

B

A

47 cm
(18¼″)

12 cm
(4¾″)

●**Quick Steps:**

1. Stand alocasia so leaf slants down from left to right.

2. Place begonia to left of stem, with flowers facing you.

18

Treasures popping out in every direction give the effect of vigorous space and depth.

Materials: Anthurium, Lady's mantle, Blazing-star
Container: Jewelry box
Others: *Kenzan* (needlepoint holder), Small glass bowl
Finished size: W 60 cm × H 24 cm
(23½″ × 9¼″)
See page 84 for arranging steps.

◆DINING ROOMS

Avoid strong scented flowers for dining rooms. Select the container according to the season, such as clear glassware for summer. Display appetizing creations to compliment your meals.

19   **The heaviness of the fruits can be softened by the airy lines of beargrass.**
Materials: Chestnuts in bur, Pomegranate, Lime, Beargrass, Globe amaranth   **Container:** Lacquered bowl
Finished size: W 36 cm × H 26 cm (11″ × 10¼″)
●**Tips:** Arrange fruits or vegetables in container. Form beargrass into circles and secure ends underneath fruits. Stand globe amaranth upright as focal point.

Playful decorations of fruits and vegetables.

20

Thin dianthuses added to fennel give a sweet and delicate impression.

Materials: Fennel, Dianthus
Container: Small serving bowl
Others: #30 wire
Finished size: W20 cm × H35 cm (8″ × 13¾″)
●Tips:
Bundle fennel into a dome shape; bind stems with wire. Trim stems to fit and place in container. Put two dianthuses upright, varying heights.

21

Cheerful harmony of cherry tomatoes and parsley enhanced with twining smilax vine.

Materials: Parsley, Cherry tomato, Smilax, Oncidium
Containers: 2 flute glasses
Finished size: W42 cm × H27 cm (16¼″ × 10½″)

Materials: Parsley (**A**), Cherry tomato (**B**), Oncidium (**C**), Smilax (**D**)

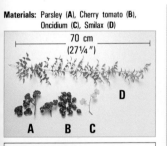

●Quick Steps:

1. Fill each glass with parsley and tomatoes, one parsley stem leaning right.

2. Draw smilax in a flowing line as shown. Add oncidium.

◆ DINING ROOMS

22

Natural beauty of cosmos can be recreated by placing them in various directions so they appear to be blown by autumn breezes.

Materials: Cosmos, Rice flower, Sprengeri, Baby's breath
Container: Compote
Others: *Kenzan* (needlepoint holder)
Finished size: W 58 cm × H 31 cm
(22½″ × 12″)
See page 85 for arranging steps.

23

Enjoy the assortment of colors and shapes of flowers nestled in tiny glass bowls.

Materials: Blue fantasy, Oncidium, Begonia, Balloonflower
Containers: Glass dish, 3 small bowls
Finished size: W 26 cm × H 9 cm
(10¼″ × 3½″)

● **Quick Steps:**

1. Place ballonflower, oncidium and begonia leaf in each glass bowl.

2. Arrange blue fantasy in good proportions for a floating look.

24

A low mass of carnations accentuated by upright growth of leaves.

Materials: Carnation, Dracaena
Container: Covered candy dish
Finished size: W 15 cm × H 22 cm
(5¾″ × 8½″)

● **Quick Steps:**

1. Place 8-9 carnations, varying each length.

2. Stand dracaena leaves upright in middle left.

25

The stern form of classic glasses is mellowed by the lines of flowing smilax and prairie gentians.

Materials: Prairie gentian, Smilax
Containers: Pair wine glasses
Finished size: W 37 cm × H 24 cm
(14½″ × 9¼″)

● **Tips:**

Cut stems of prairie gentians at an angle so it can be balanced at a low angle against inside of glass. Make an arch of smilax by securing one end in each glass.

◆LIVING ROOMS

Customize each arrangement to suit your guest's personality.

26

Long lines of leaves fresh with dew combined with a large container accentuate the expanse of flower-strewn water.

Materials: Sweetflag leaves, Hydrangea   **Container:** Salad bowl
Others: #30 wire, Weight (*kenzan*, or needlepoint holder)   **Finished size:** W 60 cm × H 18 cm (23½″ × 7″)
●**Tips:** Tie wire through a small *kenzan* using as weight. Take excess wire and bind layered 6 leaves together. Float 13 florets on water.

Arrange table flowers in a low position in balance with the dinnerware.

27

Bouquet style arrangement of pale colored lilies conveys the sweet scent.
Materials: "Le léve" lily, Elegant lily, Larkspur
Container: Salad bowl
Finished size: W 28 cm × H 21 cm (11″ × 8¼″)

●**Quick Steps:**

1. Place lilies varying lengths, resting heads on rim of container.

2. Accentuate with larkspur.

Show the best of the growing lines of branches for a breezy effect.

◆ LIVING ROOMS

 Generously extended branches give a light image in contrast with the color and the shape of the container.

Materials: Japanese beauty berry, Feather cockscomb, Ageratum **Container:** Glass vase
Finished size: W 100 cm × H 92 cm (39″ × 35¾″)
See page 86 for arranging steps.

●Quick Steps:

1. Remove leaves of prairie gentians, and combine 3 stems by binding with wire.

2. Place weeping golden bell upright in center of container, to show the best angle of its shape.

3. Add bound prairie gentians behind weeping golden bell, hiding stems.

4. Right-side view of finished arrangement.

29

Take advantage of natural shape of the branch, and express the rising strength by showing only one thick stem.

Materials: Weeping golden bell, Prairie gentian
Container: Square container
Others: *Kenzan* (needlepoint holder), #30 wire
Finished size: W 48 cm × H 80 cm (18¾″ × 31¼″)

30

Leafless stems of wisteria create simple curvy line which expand the space in front of you.

Materials: Wisteria, Hydrangea macrophylla normalis
Container: Tea tin
Others: *Kenzan* (needlepoint holder)
Finished size: W 73 cm × H 51 cm (28½″ × 20″)
See page 83 for arranging steps.

◆LIVING ROOMS

31

Striking leaves and double flowering cherry blossoms contribute to a vertical attitude.

Materials: Japanese banana plant, Double-flowering cherry blossom   **Container:** Irregular-shaped vase
Others: *Kenzan* (needlepoint holder)
Finished size: W 54 cm × H 80 cm (21″ × 31¼″)

See page 87 for arranging steps.

32 **Hosta and smilax define the shape while the white flowers express coolness.**
Materials: Hosta, Peruvian lily, Smilax
Container: Glass vase
Finished size: W 47 cm × H 49 cm (18¼″ × 19″)
See page 88 for arranging steps.

25

◆ HALLS

The hallway is the place to welcome guests. Give it a seasonal touch with elegance.

33

The gentle lines of solidaster and delicate baby's breath soften the strong mass of ixora chinensis.

Materials: Solidaster, Baby's breath, Ixora chinensis
Container: Tumbler
Others: 2 pcs 90 cm × 35 cm (35″ × 13¾″) wrapping tulle in both black and white, #30 wire
Finished size: W 62 cm × H 43 cm (24¼″ × 16¾″)
See page 89 for arranging steps.

34

The rigid and thick line of Japanese maholia sets off the thin wavering line of the flowers.

Materials: Japanese maholia, Thalictrum, Speedwell, Chrysanthemum
Container: Compote
Others: *Kenzan* (needlepoint holder)
Finished size: W 68 cm × H 63 cm (26½″ × 24½″)
See page 90 for arranging steps.

Welcome your guests with seasonal beauty.

35

A feeling of motion is achieved with the slender stems of dianthus and camellias nestled at the base.

Materials: Dianthus, Camellia
Container: Irregular-shaped vase
Others: 2 *kenzan* (needlepoint holder)
Finished size: W 44 cm × H 55 cm
(17¼″ × 21½″)
See page 89 for arranging steps.

36

Flowers assembled to express vitality in soft and fresh hues of green.

Materials: Magnolia hypoleuca, China aster, Fennel
Container: Irregular-shaped vase
Finished size: W 72 cm × H 60 cm
(28″ × 23½″)
See page 91 for arranging steps.

HALLS

37

A chic assortment featuring the delicate hues of delphiniums provides a focal point for your hall.

Materials: Delphinium, Macleaya cordata, Solidaster
Container: *Suiban* (shallow container)
Others: 2 *kenzan* (needlepoint holder)
Finished size: W 110 cm × H 65 cm (43″ × 25¼″)
See page 92 for arranging steps.

38

Fanned agapanthus and echoing lace flowers create a refreshing look.

Materials: African lily, Lace flower, Wax tree
Container: Irregular-shaped vase
Others: 2 *kenzan* (needlepoint holder)
Finished size: W 80 cm × H 57 cm (31¼″ × 22¼″)
See page 93 for arranging steps.

39

The dynamic lines of allium schubertii together with glory lilies give a striking impression.

Materials: Allium schubertii, Glory lily, Smilax
Container: Irregular-shaped vase
Finished size: W 60 cm × H 67 cm
(23½″ × 26¼″)

See page 94 for arranging steps.

40

Create a naturally flowing line with a massed florets of kaffir lily as the focal point.

Materials: Satsuma mock orangre, Kaffir lily
Container: Tube-shaped vase
Finished size: W 75 cm × H 50 cm
(29¼″ × 19½″)

See page 95 for arranging steps.

41 **The same materials are arranged in different ways for a tiered effect.**

Materials: Fern, Spray mum, Small chrysanthemum, Stenophyllum
Containers: 3 tumblers
Others: #30 wire
Finished size: Top: W56 cm × H27 cm (21¾″ × 10½″)
  Middle: W57 cm × H31 cm (22¼″ × 12″)
  Bottom: W67 cm × H39 cm (26¼″ × 15½″)
See page 96 for arranging steps.

42

The dramatic vertical lines of the Japanese bulrush express definition and suggest a cool breeze.

Materials: Japanese bulrush, Alpine rose, Iris leaf
Container: Glass vase
Others: *Kenzan* (needlepoint holder)
Finished size: W 50 cm × H 110 cm (19½″ × 43″)
See page 97 for arranging steps.

43

The straight lines of the Japanese bulrush are contrasted with selloum creating a delicate light reflection.

Materials: Japanese bulrush, Baby's breath, Selloum
Container: Glass vase
Finished size: W 85 cm × H 95 cm (33¼″ × 37″)
See page 97 for arranging steps.

◆ BATHROOMS

The bathroom is a place for relaxation. Give it a freshness to enliven you in the morning or evening. Make a simple arrangement for this small room.

44 Take delicate lace flowers and add spirit with two bulrush stalks.

Materials: Japanese bulrush, Lace flower, Scabiosa
Container: Tumbler
Finished size: W 32 cm × H 61 cm (12½″ × 23¾″)
●**Tips:** Cross stems of lace flower and scabiosa in container. Insert Japanese bulrush slanting toward left.

Keep "Naturally and Simply" in mind when arranging for a small area.

45

Fill the glass with water and indulge the curvy lines of the foliage. Take advantage of the lens effect.

Materials: Dracaena, Rose
Container: Goblet
Finished size: W 11 cm × H 24 cm (4½″ × 9¼″)

●**Tips:**
Curl leaf and set it in water. Slant rose toward front left, securing cut stem edge inside of goblet.

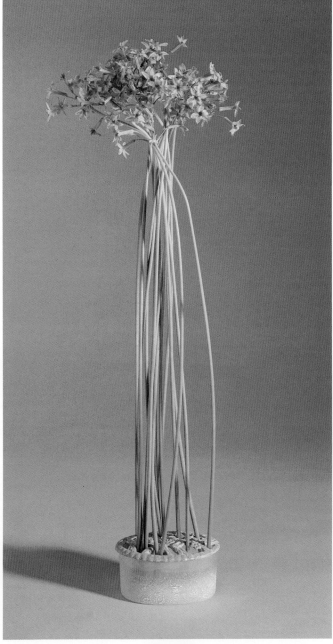

46

Utilizing the lattice of the potpourri pot, stand the long-stems of the sweet garlic. Cross the tops to give an assembled look.

Material: Sweet garlic
Container: Potpourri pot
Finished size: W 18 cm × H 50 cm (7″ × 19½″)

●**Tips:**
Show beauty of stalks. Insert a few stalks in each square and stabilize upper sections by crossing each other.

◆ JAPANESE ROOMS

The intimacy of woven mats and the vertical lines of a Japanese room can look quite different with a careful choice of flowers and displaying area. Create a calm and relaxed atmosphere to make everyone feel at home.

47 Create a modern aspect in your Japanese room by arranging tall allium giganteum. This gives an artistic effect.

Materials: Japanese banana plant, Allium giganteum, Blue fantasy, Asparagus fern   **Container:** *Suiban* (shallow container)
Others: *Kenzan* (needlepoint holder), Pebbles   **Finished size:** W 93 cm × H 88 cm (36½″ × 34¼″)
See page 98 for arranging steps.

A dignified style most suited to *tokonoma* (alcove).

48

Trim the leaves of satsuma mock orangre to highlight the beautiful shape of its stems.

Materials: Satsuma mock orangre, Hosta, Prairie gentian, Peruvian lily
Container: Tube-shaped vase
Others: #30 wire
Finished size: W 56 cm × H 72 cm
(21¾″ × 28″)
See page 99 for arranging steps.

49

The delicate cascading lines of beargrass contrast well with the central white flowers.

Materials: Beargrass, Peony, Candytuft
Container: *Suiban* (shallow container)
Others: *Kenzan* (needlepoint holder), #30 wire
Finished size: W 86 cm × H 59 cm
(33½″ × 23″)
See page 100 for arranging steps.

◆JAPANESE ROOMS

50

The classic, intricate lines of billberry are softened by smokegrass to express summer coolness.

Materials: Billberry, Smokegrass, Ageratum
Container: Tea box
Others: *Kenzan* (needlepoint holder), Small vessel
Finished size: W 52 cm × H 54 cm (20¼″ × 21″)
See page 101 for arranging steps.

51

A fragile elegance expressed by asparagus and balloonflower, one of the "Seven Flowers of Autumn".

Materials: Baloonflower, Asparagus fern
Container: Basket with inner vessel
Others: *Kenzan* (needlepoint holder)
Finished size: W 34 cm × H 30 cm (13¼″ × 11¾″)

32 cm
(12½″)

B

A

Materials: Balloonflower (**A**), Asparagus fern (**B**)

1. Arrange balloonflowers from front, slanting a little left.

2. Utilizing natural shape, add asparagus fern from front.

3. Spread fern so that the longest stem falls below rim of container.

◆ JAPANESE ROOMS

53

Let the bridal wreath inscribe flowing lines in the air. A pink camellia provides focal point.

Materials: Bridal wreath, Camellia
Container: Small bowl
Others: *Kenzan* (needlepoint holder), Pebbles
Finished size: W 43 cm × H 63 cm (16¾″ × 24½″)

52

The brilliance of orange peonies enchanted by graceful arrow-wood branches.

Materials: Arrowwood, Peony
Container: Basket
Others: 2 *kenzan* (needlepoint holder), 2 small vessels
Finished size: W 92 cm × H 74 cm (35¾″ × 28¾″)

See page 102 for arranging steps.

● **Quick Steps:**

1. Put camellia in center of container, inclining forward.

2. Stand bridal wreath upright behind camellia.

3. Right-side view: camellia is slanting forward.

54

**Delicate spirea combined with balloon-
flowers makes a chic, restrained image.**

Materials: Spirea, Balloonflower
Container: Tube-shaped vase
Finished size: W 56 cm × H 73 cm
(21¼″ × 28½″)
See page 103 for arranging steps.

55

**Place two containers either at
the front/back or left/right
to create depth and dimen-
tion.**

Materials: Mountain laurel, Calla lily
Containers: 2 *suiban* (shallow container)
Others: 2 *kenzan* (needlepoint holder)
Finished size: Left: W 55 cm × H 40 cm
(21½″ × 15½″)
Right: W 41 cm × H 26 cm
(16″ × 10¼″)
See page 104 for arranging steps.

ARRANGING WILD GRASSES

◆ KNOTWEED

75 cm
(29¾")

56

Tiny red florets are playing with each other in the air.

Materials: Knotweed   **Containers:** 2 planters
Others: 2 *kenzan* (needlepoint holder)
Finished size: W 78 cm × H 65 cm (30½" × 25¼")

●**Quick Steps:**

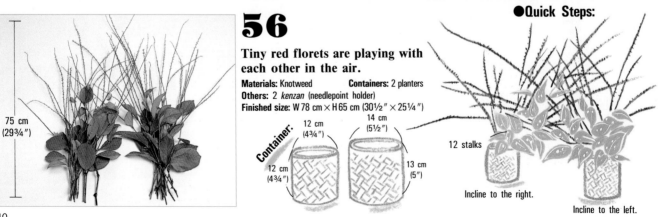

Container.

12 cm
(4¾")

14 cm
(5½")

12 cm
(4¾")

13 cm
(5")

Planters

12 stalks

Incline to the right.

Incline to the left.

Wild flowers gathered from the field will reproduce a sense of Nature in your home. Arrange them freely or use a little technique to highlight the features of the various flowers. Enjoy the sweet fragrances of outdoors.

◆ SAURURACEAE

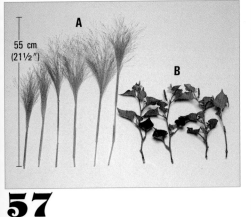

A

B

55 cm
(21½″)

57

Silently blooming white flowers combined with smokegrass make a vital, fresh atmosphere.

Materials: Smokegrass (**A**), Saururaceae (**B**)
Containers: Plant pot
Others: *Kenzan* (needlepoint holder)
Finished size: W 20 cm × H 57 cm (7″ × 22¼″)

Rear view   Right-side view

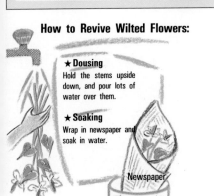

How to Revive Wilted Flowers:

★ **Dousing**
Hold the stems upside down, and pour lots of water over them.

★ **Soaking**
Wrap in newspaper and soak in water.

Newspaper

Container:
11 cm
(4½″)

10 cm
(4″)

Plant pot

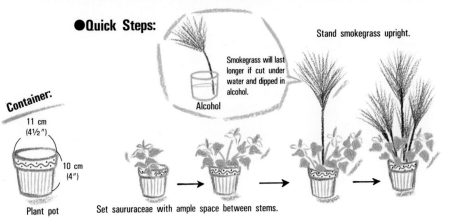

● **Quick Steps:**

Smokegrass will last longer if cut under water and dipped in alcohol.

Alcohol

Stand smokegrass upright.

Set saururaceae with ample space between stems.

◆ GREENBRIER

A

B

57 cm
(22¼")

58

With vividly colored containers, the striking lines of greenbrier are evident.

Materials: Greenbrier (**A**), Hordeum murinum (**B**)
Containers: 2 milk cartons
Others: Colored *washi* paper, # 30 wire
Finished size: W 86 cm × H 50 cm
(33½" × 19½")

Arrange several twigs using their natural shapes.

● **Quick Steps:**

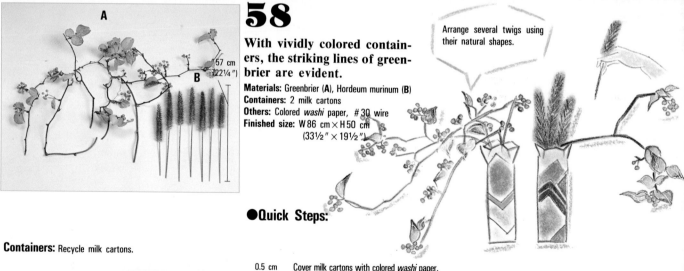

Containers: Recycle milk cartons.

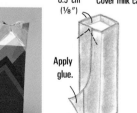

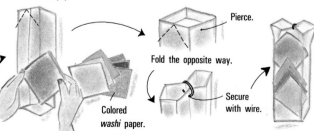

0.5 cm
(⅛")

Cover milk cartons with colored *washi* paper.

Apply glue.

Colored *washi* paper.

Pierce.

Fold the opposite way.

Secure with wire.

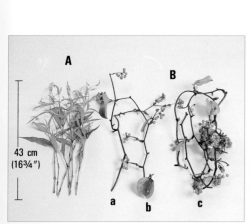

59

**Plants under water. Arrange loosely in a
clear vase.**

Materials: Polygonum longisetum (**A**), Greenbrier (**B**)
Containers: Glass vase
Finished size: W 62 cm × H 57 cm
(24¼″ × 22½″)

●**Quick Steps:**

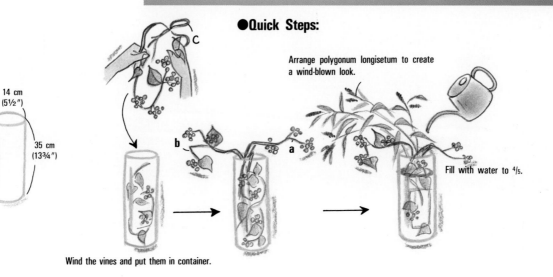

Arrange polygonum longisetum to create
a wind-blown look.

Fill with water to ⁴/₅.

Wind the vines and put them in container.

◆ GREAT BURNET

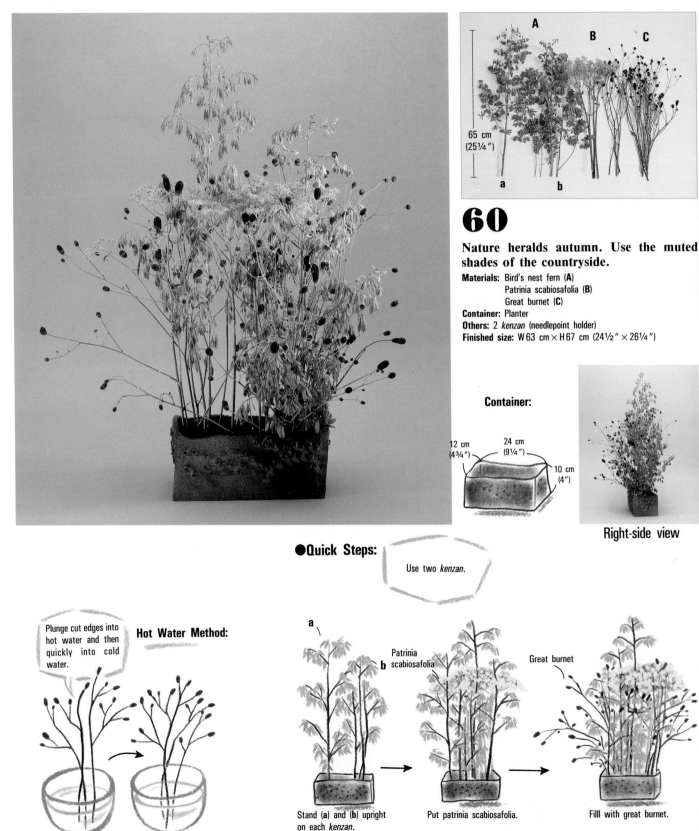

A · B · C

65 cm
(25¼″)

a   b

60

Nature heralds autumn. Use the muted shades of the countryside.

Materials: Bird's nest fern (**A**)
Patrinia scabiosafolia (**B**)
Great burnet (**C**)
Container: Planter
Others: 2 *kenzan* (needlepoint holder)
Finished size: W 63 cm × H 67 cm (24½″ × 26¼″)

Container:

12 cm
(4¾″)   24 cm
(9¼″)

10 cm
(4″)

Right-side view

● **Quick Steps:**

Use two *kenzan*.

Hot Water Method:

Plunge cut edges into hot water and then quickly into cold water.

Hot water   Cold water

a

Patrinia
b scabiosafolia

Great burnet

Stand (**a**) and (**b**) upright
on each *kenzan*.

Put patrinia scabiosafolia.

Filll with great burnet.

61

Wild flowers mingled with grasses. Great burnet and kangaroo grass are added for volume.

Materials: Kangaroo grass (**A**)
　　　　　Great burnet (**B**)
　　　　　Japanese knotwood (**C**)
Container: Traditional stationery box
Others: *Kenzan* (needlepoint holder)
　　　　Small vessel
Finished size: W 67 cm × H 47 cm
　　　　　　　(26¼″ × 18¼″)

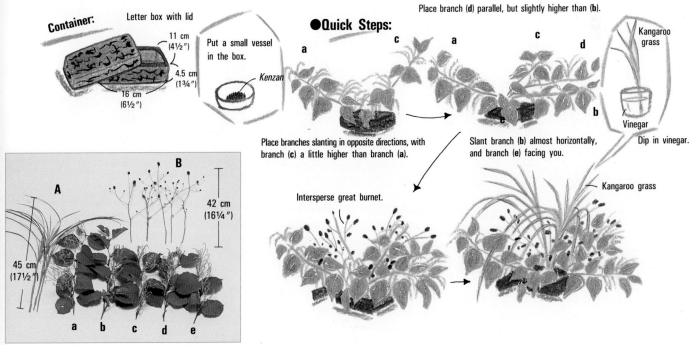

Container:

Letter box with lid

11 cm (4½″)

4.5 cm (1¾″)

16 cm (6½″)

Put a small vessel in the box.

Kenzan

Place branch (d) parallel, but slightly higher than (b).

●**Quick Steps:**

a

c　　a　　c　　d

Kangaroo grass

b

Vinegar

Dip in vinegar.

Place branches slanting in opposite directions, with branch (c) a little higher than branch (a).

Slant branch (b) almost horizontally, and branch (e) facing you.

Interperse great burnet.

Kangaroo grass

B

A

42 cm (16¼″)

45 cm (17½″)

a　b　c　d　e

◆ FOXTAIL

62

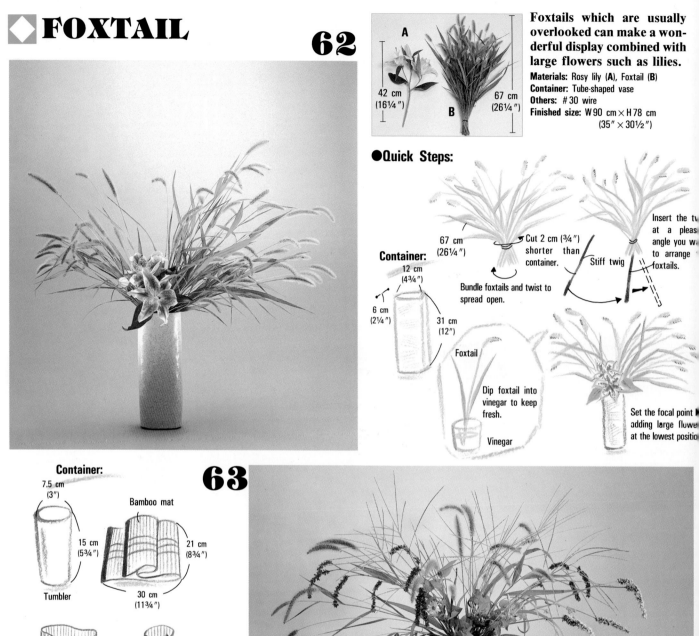

Foxtails which are usually overlooked can make a wonderful display combined with large flowers such as lilies.

Materials: Rosy lily (**A**), Foxtail (**B**)
Container: Tube-shaped vase
Others: #30 wire
Finished size: W 90 cm × H 78 cm
(35″ × 30½″)

A
42 cm
(16¼″)

B
67 cm
(26¼″)

● **Quick Steps:**

Container:
12 cm
(4¾″)

6 cm
(2¼″)

31 cm
(12″)

67 cm
(26¼″)

Cut 2 cm (¾″) shorter than container.

Bundle foxtails and twist to spread open.

Stiff twig

Insert the tw
at a pleas
angle you wa
to arrange
foxtails.

Foxtail

Dip foxtail into vinegar to keep fresh.

Vinegar

Set the focal point
adding large flowe
at the lowest positio

63

Container:
7.5 cm
(3″)

15 cm
(5¾″)

Tumbler

Bamboo mat

21 cm
(8¾″)

30 cm
(11¾″)

Secure with wire.

Wrap with mat.

Arrange to give a softly spread-out impression.

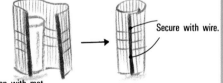

A
B
C
D E F

63 cm
(24½″)

Red hues that are the most striking in Nature are featured here. Spread widely for a soft impression.

Materials: Foxtail (**A**), Polygonum orientale (**B**), Crabgrass (**C**), Aster (**D**), Evening primrose (**E**), Sonchus asper (**F**)
Containers: Tumbler, Bamboo mat
Others: #30 wire
Finished size: W 68 cm × H 58 cm
(26½″ × 22½″)

◆ JAPANESE PAMPAS

64

Japanese pampas, a typical autumn tassel, salute from among grasses to create a rustic, heart-warming image.

Materials: Japanese pampas (**A**)
Patrinia scabiosafolia and Shepherd's purse (**B**)
Polygonum longisetum (**C**)
Container: Bamboo colandar
Others: *Kenzan* (needlepoint holder), Small vessel
Finished size: W 86 cm × H 44 cm (33½″ × 17¼″)

A   B   C

68 cm
(26½″)

Container:
36 cm
(14″)   Bamboo colandar

11 cm
(4½″)

Cut under water and dip into vinegar to keep fresh.

Japanese pampas

Vinegar

●Quick Steps:

Arrange a generous amount of flowers in a dome shape.

Add polygonum longisetum spaciously to create depth.

Insert Japanese pampas slanting low for a wind-blown effect.

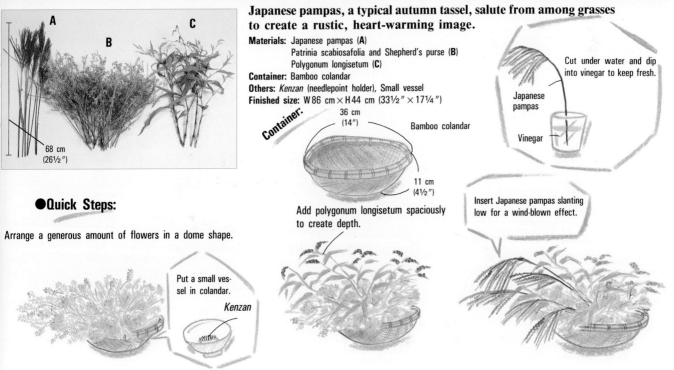

Put a small vessel in colandar.

Kenzan

FESTIVE ARRANGEMENTS

◆ NEW YEAR'S

Pine, bamboo, and plum are the typical materials for the New Year, but you can freely create a classic or modern image depending on the flowers you choose.

65

Traditional trio of pine, bamboo and plum can make a bold impression by adding yellow and orange flowers.

Materials: *Janome* pine, Lichened plum branch, Bird-of-paradise, Bamboo, Oncidium
Containers: *Suiban* (shallow container)
Others: Red/white and silver/gold *mizuhiki* (paper cord), *Kenzan* (needlepoint holder), #30 wire
Finished size: W 81 cm × H 47 cm (31½" × 18¼")

See page 106 for arranging steps.

Even the busiest person feels like displaying flowers for festive occasions such as Christmas or New Year. The following are celebration arrangements suitable for each occasion, simple enough for beginners.

Formal and modern arrangements with pine, the theme material for the New Year.

66 **Variegated pine and ilex are magnificently assembled to create a dramatic impression.**
Materials: Ilex, *Janome* pine, Small chrysanthemum
Container: Irregular-shaped vase
Finished size: W 62 cm × H 46 cm (24¼″ × 18″)

See page 105 for arranging steps.

Fresh, contemporary arrangements to welcome the New Year.

◆ NEW YEAR'S

67 The Goddess of Spring is said to dwell in pine trees for the new year to bring happiness to all. Add pastel tones to the evergreen leaves to express a fresh beginning.

Materials: Pine, Rose, Blue fantasy   **Container:** *Suiban* (shallow container)
Others: *Kenzan* (needlepoint holder)   **Finished size:** W 68 cm × H 36 cm (26½″ × 14″)

See page 107 for arranging steps.

68

An image of youth created with long leaf pine and delicate freesias.

Materials: Long leaf pine, Freesia
Containers: 2 narrow rectangular vases
Others: 28 cm × 11 cm (11″ × 4½″) chiken wire, #30 wire
Finished size: W 72 cm × H 40 cm
(28″ × 15½″)
See page 108 for arranging steps.

69

This bold arrangement shows each material to its best. Red and white, silver and gold *mizuhiki* (paper cords) add up to a festive mood.

Materials: Long leaf pine, Lichened plum branch, Lobster claw
Container: Square vase
Others: *Kenzan* (needlepoint holder), *Mizuhiki* (paper cord), #30 wire
Finished size: W 97 cm × H 60 cm
(37¾″ × 23½″)
See page 109 for arranging steps.

◆ NEW YEAR'S

70 The green color of pine is enhanced by the red and white of the anthrium and baby's breath. Suitable for a Western-style room.

Materials: Young pine, Anthurium, Baby's breath   **Container:** Irregular-shaped vase
Others: *Kenzan* (needlepoint holder)   **Finished size:** W 45 cm × H 63 cm (17½″ × 24½″)   See page 110 for arranging steps.

71

Artistic New Year display, using traditional materials such as pine, plum and red berries.

Materials: Pine, Lichened plum branch, Rosehip
Container: *Hagoita*-shaped lacquered tray
Others: *Oibane* (shuttlecock), Silver and gold *mizuhiki* (paper cords), #30 wire
Finished size: W 24 cm × H 60 cm
(9¼″ × 23½″)
See page 113 for arranging steps.

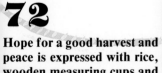

72

Hope for a good harvest and peace is expressed with rice, wooden measuring cups and spray mums.

Materials: Pine, Small chrysanthemum (pink, yellow), Ear of rice
Containers: 3 wooden measuring cups, *Kaiseki-bon* (lacquered tray)
Finished size: W 80 cm × H 20 cm
(31¼″ × 7″)
See page 113 for arranging steps.

◆ THE DOLL FESTIVAL — March 3rd

On the 3rd day of the 3rd month of the year, Japanese parents and grandparents celebrate the healthy growth of their little girls with traditional dolls and food. An antique doll set may be handed down to the daughter, or a brand-new set may be given.

73

A sweet arrangement suggesting that spring is just around the corner.

Materials: Myriocladus, Delta maidenhair fern, Peach blossom (silk flower), Butterfly ornament
Container: Glass salad bowl
Others: *Kenzan* (needlepoint holder), Florist's foam
Finished size: W 36 cm × H 47 cm
(14″ × 18¼″)
See page 119 for arranging steps.

Festive arrangements celebrate children's healthy growth.

◆BOYS' DAY—May 5th

The 5th day of the 5th month of the year is a day to celebrate the little boys' growth, displaying warrior dolls inside the home and carp streamers outside. Sweetflag or sword-leaved iris is traditionally used so that the boy will likewise grow tall and strong.

75

It is important to hide the flower stems by varying the heights and the directions of leaves.

Materials: Sweetflag
Container: Small bowl
Others: Kenzan (needlepoint holder)
Finished size: W 38 cm × H 70 cm (14¾" × 27¼")
●**Tips:** Position the flowers first, then fill with leaves, not higher than flowers. See page 111 (no. 74) for more details.

74

Sword-leaved iris is the symbol of the Boys' day. *Suiban* (container) lets the beautiful surface of the water show.

Materials: Sweetflag, Spirea
Container: *Suiban* (shallow container)
Others: 2 *kenzan* (needlepoint holder)
Finished size: W 77 cm × H 82 cm
(30" × 32")
See page 111 for arranging steps.

76

A single iris leaf "stands" straight and tall for parents' wish for their children.

Materials: Clematis, Iris leaf
Container: Vase
Finished size: W 21 cm × H 59 cm
(8¼" × 23")
See page 113 for arranging steps.

◆ MOTHER'S DAY — 2nd Sunday of May

Carnations will say more when handed with the words "Thank you."

77

Wrap a bunch of pure red carnations in a special way. See page 112 for arranging steps.

78

The red color of carnations is highlighted with white florets of dianthus and baby's breath.

Materials: Carnation, Dianthus, Baby's breath
Container: Irregular-shaped vase
Others: *Kenzan* (needlepoint holder)
Finished size: W 51 cm × H 52 cm
(20″ × 20¼″)
See page 116 for arranging steps.

Enhance the enjoyment with a heartwarming arrangement.

◆ MOON-VIEWING PARTY — Mid-September

This custom was originated from farmers' religious observances to ensure a good harvest. In the middle of September, homemade dumplings, seasonal fruit and vegetables are offered to the full moon, while appreciating its beauty. Japanese pampas is a must for this display.

79

Add colors to Japanese pampas to create a taste of autumn.

Materials: Japanese pampas, Patrinia scabiosafolia, Polygonum orientale
Container: Bamboo basket with inner vessel
Others: Miniature *kenzan* (needlepoint holder)
Finished size: W 42 cm × H 75 cm
(16¼" × 29¼")

See page 103 for arranging steps.

◆CHRISTMAS

Preparing for Christmas is always exciting even though it is the busiest time of the year. Do your flower arrangements early, and you will feel uplifted and joyous whenever you see them.

Gold Arrangement   Silver Arrangement

80 The colors of candles echo the gilded holly, reflect the flame and enhance the basic red and green pairing.

Materials: Holly, Poinsettia, Rosehip

Containers: 2 *suiban* (shallow container)

Others: 2 candles (silver and gold), Spray paint (silver and gold), Angel-hair, 2 *kenzan* (needlepoint holder)

Finished size: W 110 cm × H 38 cm (43″ × 14¾″)

See page 118 for arranging steps.

Celebrate the season with red, green, glitter and candles.

81 **Freestyle Christmas wreath with silver-tinted holly and red berries.**
Materials: Holly, Greenbrier
Others: Diam 36 cm (14″) wreath, Ribbon, Christmas balls, Small bell
Finished size: W 52 cm × H 75 cm (20¼″ × 29¼″)
See page 114 for arranging steps.

◆ CHRISTMAS

82 **Modernize the classic image of Japanese winterberry with glittering iridescent tinsel.**

Materials: Japanese winterberry, Poinsettia
Container: Narrow rectangular vase
Others: Iridescent tinsel
Finished size: W 72 cm × H 53 cm (28″ × 20½″)
See page 115 for arranging steps.

83

A single branch of fir will make a dynamic impression paired with a mass of red berries.

Materials: Fir, Mountain ash berry
Container: Basket with handle
Others: Ribbon, Small bells, 2 *kenzan* (needlepoint holder), Small vessel, #30 wire
Finished size: W 78 cm × H 66 cm (30½″ × 25¾″)
See page 122 for arranging steps.

◆BIRTHDAY

Arrange his/her favorite flowers in a cheerful style. The fragrance will fill the room and liven the atmosphere.

Fun arrangements for the fun day.

84 Distinctive style in a fresh pastel. Insert your birthday card for a heartwarming wish.

Materials: Amacrinum lily, Spider plant, Curly fern   **Container:** Irregular-shaped vase   **Others:** Birthday card
Finished size: W 52 cm × H 50 cm (20¼″ × 19½″)
See page 117 for arranging steps.

85

A dazzling display of roses and miniature roses with depth and dimension. When arranging a number of flowers, remove excess leaves to highlight the stems.

Materials: Rose (red, custard)
 Miniature rose (pink, yellow)
Container: Irregular-shaped vase
Finished size: W 74 cm × H 59 cm
 (28¾″ × 23″)

See page 120 for arranging steps.

◆ WEDDING ANNIVERSARY

How about a romantic home-cooked dinner for two? A bottle of your favorite wine and flowers on the table will make an unforgettable memory.

87

Create a soft and sweet image with pastel toned flowers and curvy greens.

Materials: Weeping golden bell, Spirea, Oriental hybrid lily, Rosy lily, Baby's breath, Beargrass
Container: Irregular shaped vase
Finished size: W 113 cm × H 65 cm (44″ × 25¼″)
See page 121 for arranging steps.

86

Simply put a wide-spread branch of orchid and lobster claw in a decorative decanter.

Materials: Oncidium, Lobster claw, Asparagus fern
Container: Decanter
Finished size: W 47 cm × H 48 cm (18¼″ × 18¾″)
See page 112 for arranging steps.

Express your love and thanks with a floral composition.

MASTERING BASIC STYLES

◆ UPRIGHT STYLE (*Moribana*)

This is the most basic structure in ikebana. Easy-to-handle weeping golden bell and roses are arranged in a round *suiban* (shallow container).

88

WHAT IS *MORIBANA*?

Moribana literally means "piled-up flowers", which are arranged in a shallow container such as *suiban*, compote or basket. *Moribana* is secured on *kenzan*, or needlepoint holder(s).

Learn the ikebana concept of shape and space through three basic styles: "Upright style", "Slanting style" and "Cascading style".

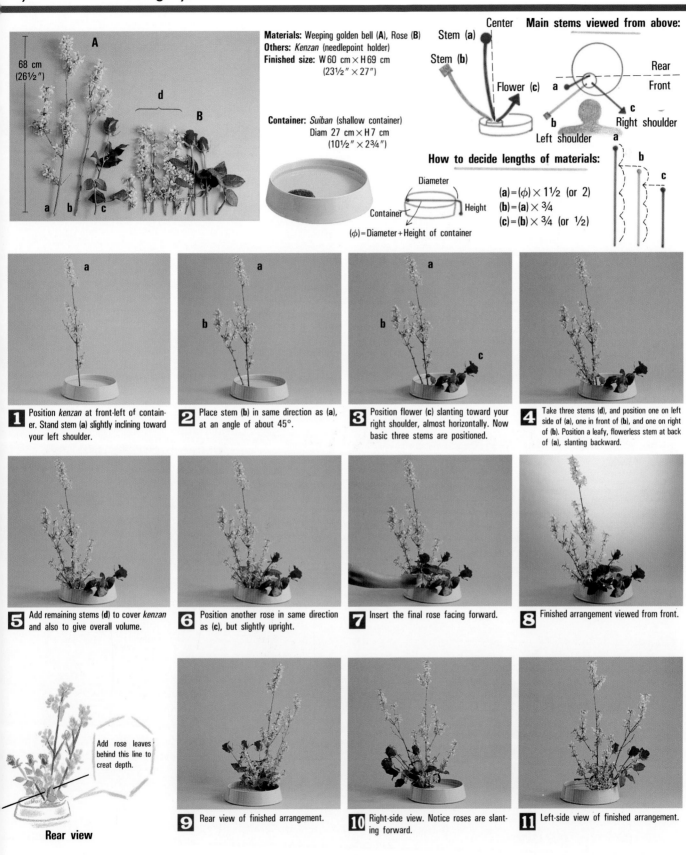

Materials: Weeping golden bell (**A**), Rose (**B**)
Others: *Kenzan* (needlepoint holder)
Finished size: W 60 cm × H 69 cm
  (23½″ × 27″)

Container: *Suiban* (shallow container)
  Diam 27 cm × H 7 cm
  (10½″ × 2¾″)

68 cm
(26½″)

Center
Stem (a)
Stem (b)
Flower (c)

Main stems viewed from above:
Rear
Front
Right shoulder
Left shoulder

How to decide lengths of materials:

Diameter
Height
Container
(φ) = Diameter + Height of container

(**a**) = (φ) × 1½ (or 2)
(**b**) = (**a**) × ¾
(**c**) = (**b**) × ¾ (or ½)

1 Position *kenzan* at front-left of container. Stand stem (**a**) slightly inclining toward your left shoulder.

2 Place stem (**b**) in same direction as (**a**), at an angle of about 45°.

3 Position flower (**c**) slanting toward your right shoulder, almost horizontally. Now basic three stems are positioned.

4 Take three stems (**d**), and position one on left side of (**a**), one in front of (**b**), and one on right of (**b**). Position a leafy, flowerless stem at back of (**a**), slanting backward.

5 Add remaining stems (**d**) to cover *kenzan* and also to give overall volume.

6 Position another rose in same direction as (**c**), but slightly upright.

7 Insert the final rose facing forward.

8 Finished arrangement viewed from front.

Add rose leaves behind this line to creat depth.

Rear view

9 Rear view of finished arrangement.

10 Right-side view. Notice roses are slanting forward.

11 Left-side view of finished arrangement.

◆UPRIGHT STYLE *(Nageire)*

89

WHAT IS *NAGEIRE*?

Nageire literally means "tossed-in flowers", which are arranged in a tall container without using *kenzan*, or needlepoint holder(s).

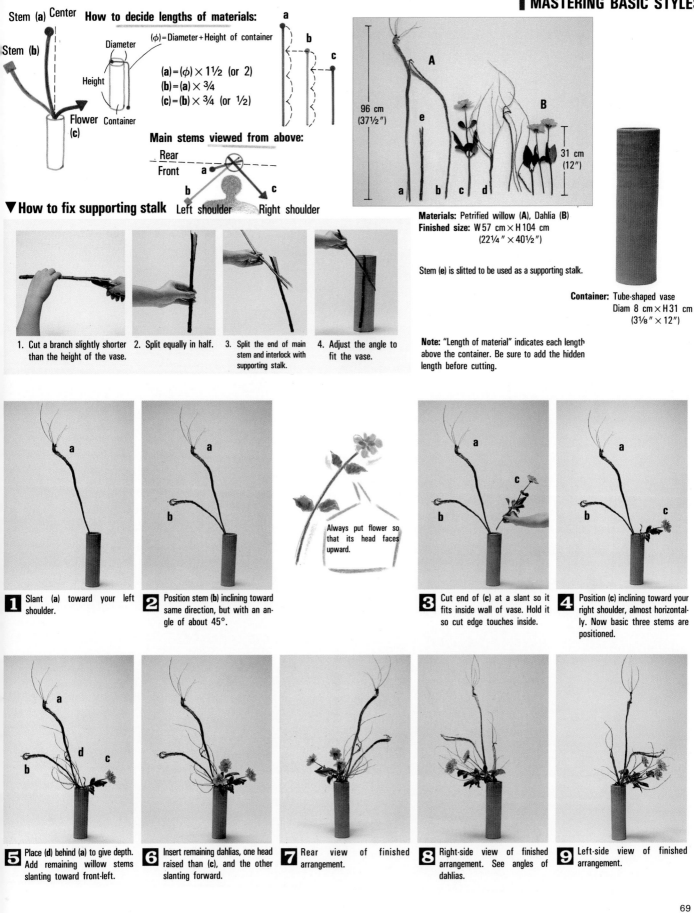

How to decide lengths of materials:

Stem (a) Center
Stem (b)
Flower (c)

Diameter
Height
Container

(ϕ) = Diameter + Height of container

(a) = $(\phi) \times 1\frac{1}{2}$ (or 2)
(b) = (a) $\times \frac{3}{4}$
(c) = (b) $\times \frac{3}{4}$ (or $\frac{1}{2}$)

a
b
c

Main stems viewed from above:

Rear
Front
a
b
c
Left shoulder   Right shoulder

▼ How to fix supporting stalk

1. Cut a branch slightly shorter than the height of the vase.
2. Split equally in half.
3. Split the end of main stem and interlock with supporting stalk.
4. Adjust the angle to fit the vase.

96 cm (37½")
A
e
B
31 cm (12")
a b c d

Materials: Petrified willow (**A**), Dahlia (**B**)
Finished size: W 57 cm × H 104 cm (22¼" × 40½")

Stem (e) is slitted to be used as a supporting stalk.

Container: Tube-shaped vase
Diam 8 cm × H 31 cm (3⅛" × 12")

Note: "Length of material" indicates each length above the container. Be sure to add the hidden length before cutting.

1 Slant (**a**) toward your left shoulder.

2 Position stem (**b**) inclining toward same direction, but with an angle of about 45°.

Always put flower so that its head faces upward.

3 Cut end of (**c**) at a slant so it fits inside wall of vase. Hold it so cut edge touches inside.

4 Position (**c**) inclining toward your right shoulder, almost horizontally. Now basic three stems are positioned.

5 Place (**d**) behind (**a**) to give depth. Add remaining willow stems slanting toward front-left.

6 Insert remaining dahlias, one head raised than (**c**), and the other slanting forward.

7 Rear view of finished arrangement.

8 Right-side view of finished arrangement. See angles of dahlias.

9 Left-side view of finished arrangement.

◆ SLANTING STYLE (*Moribana*)

The reversed arranging style can be also used depending on the placement of the display, or the shapes of branches.

90

Choose branches which look beautiful when slanted. This style will give a softer impression than the upright version.

Center

Stem (a) Stem (b)

Flower (c)

Main stems viewed from above:

Rear

Front

b

a

c

Left shoulder   Right shoulder

How to decide lengths of materials:

Diameter

Container   Height

(ϕ) = Diameter + Height of container

a

b

c

$(a) = (\phi) \times 1\frac{1}{2}$
$(b) = (a) \times \frac{3}{4}$
$(c) = (b) \times \frac{3}{4}$ (or $\frac{1}{2}$)

A

B

B

C

B

63 cm
(24½")

a   b   c

Materials: Pear bush (**A**), "Le léve" lily (**B**),
Elegant lily (**C**)
Others: *Kenzan* (needlepoint holder)
Finished size: W 68 cm × H 46 cm
(26½" × 18")
Container: *Suiban* (shallow container)
36 cm (14") in diam.

1 Position *kenzan* at back right. Place stem (a) slanting toward your left shoulder with an angle of about 45°.

2 Place (b) toward your left shoulder, almost upright.

3 Position (c) slanting toward your right shoulder, almost horizontally at 75° to 80°. Now basic three stems are positioned.

4 Add shorter stems of pear bush, at front and back of (a), slanting the same.

5 Using remaining pear bush, cover *kenzan* so as to give fullness.

6 Place 2 lilies, varying lengths, one on left side of (c), the other behind.

7 Add remaining lily stem in center, slanting forward.

8 Finished arrangement.

9 Rear view of finished arrangement.

10 Right-side view of finished arrangement. Notice positions and angles of lilies.

11 Left-side view of finished arrangement.

Each kind of lily has its own attitude:
Some flower heads face upright such as the elegant lily, some face downward like the showy lily, and some face forward like the oriental hybrid lily. Always check the direction when arranging.

◆ SLANTING STYLE (Nageire)

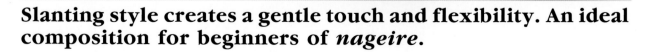

Slanting style creates a gentle touch and flexibility. An ideal composition for beginners of *nageire*.

Center

Stem (b)

Stem (a)

Flower (c)

Main stems viewed from above:

b

Rear

Front

a

c

Left shoulder   Right shoulder

How to decide lengths of materials:

Diameter

(ϕ) = Diameter + Height of container

Height

Container

$(a) = (\phi) \times 1\frac{1}{2}$

$(b) = (a) \times \frac{3}{4}$

$(c) = (b) \times \frac{3}{4}$ (or $\frac{1}{2}$)

A

B

68 cm (26½")

a   b   c

13 cm (5")

Materials: Clethra barvinervis (**A**),
Hydrangea (**B**)

Finished size: W 60 cm × H 78 cm
(23½" × 30½")

a

b

c

Container: Tube-shaped vase
Diam 7 cm × H 29 cm
(2¾" × 11¼")

Note: "Length of material" indicates
each length above the container. Be
sure to add the hidden length before
cutting.

Cross-bar fixture:

Use strong and flexible branch.

Container

Cut at a slant.   Branch   Make two.

Cut both bars slightly longer than the inner rim of the
vase, so they are secured.

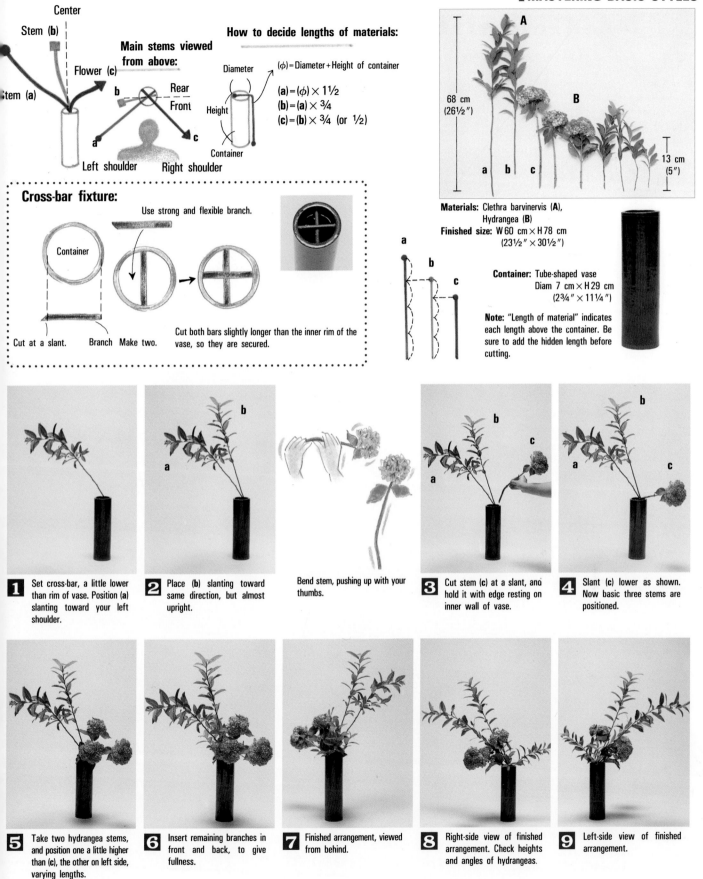

1 Set cross-bar, a little lower
than rim of vase. Position (**a**)
slanting toward your left
shoulder.

2 Place (**b**) slanting toward
same direction, but almost
upright.

Bend stem, pushing up with your
thumbs.

3 Cut stem (**c**) at a slant, and
hold it with edge resting on
inner wall of vase.

4 Slant (**c**) lower as shown.
Now basic three stems are
positioned.

5 Take two hydrangea stems,
and position one a little higher
than (**c**), the other on left side,
varying lengths.

6 Insert remaining branches in
front and back, to give
fullness.

7 Finished arrangement, viewed
from behind.

8 Right-side view of finished
arrangement. Check heights
and angles of hydrangeas.

9 Left-side view of finished
arrangement.

◆CASCADING STYLE (*Nageire*)

In this style, the main stem hangs lower than the rim of the vase. The natural curve of the spirea is emphasized with sweet pink marguerite mums in the example below.

92

Choose a flexible material which creates beautiful lines balancing with flowers.

Center

Flower (b)

Stem (a)

Main stems viewed from above:

Rear
Front

b

a

Left shoulder

Right shoulder

How to decide lengths of materials:

Diameter

(ϕ) = Diameter + Height of container

Height

$(a) = (\phi) \times 1\frac{1}{2}$

$(b) = (a) \times \frac{1}{2}, \frac{1}{3}$

Container

a

b

Note: "Length of material" indicates each length above the container. Be sure to add the hidden length before cutting.

MASTERING BASIC STYLES

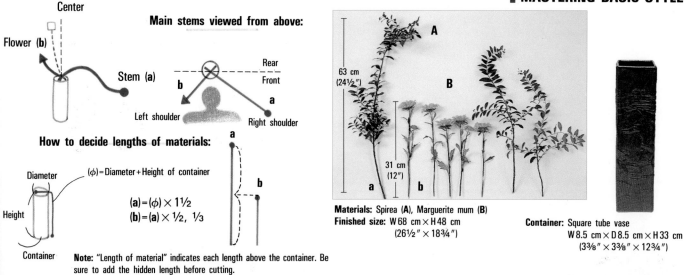

A

B

63 cm
(24½")

31 cm
(12")

a

b

Materials: Spirea (**A**), Marguerite mum (**B**)
Finished size: W 68 cm × H 48 cm
(26½" × 18¾")

Container: Square tube vase
W 8.5 cm × D 8.5 cm × H 33 cm
(3⅜" × 3⅜" × 12¾")

Holding middle and end of stem, push them against each other to ensure the best shape.

Be careful when shaping branches because some are bendable, but others are not.

Try to use the natural curve, but you can shape the stem by bending it with your hands.

Marguerite mum will settle if the stem is bent enough: Put your hands close to each other and hold the stem between the sides of forefingers and thumbs; press firmly (until the cellular texture is broken).

1 Position stem (**a**) so that cut edge rests on inside of vase and tip falls below rim, toward front right.

2 Cut stem of (**b**) diagonally resting cut edge on inner wall, position head toward your left shoulder.

3 Now two basic stems (**a**) and (**b**) are settled.

4 Put one stem of spirea at front. Put another stem behind (**a**), so it flows toward right.

5 Place marguerite mums so they slant forward, varying each height.

6 Insert remaining spirea behind flowers so it flows toward left.

7 Rear view of finished arrangement.

8 Right-side view of finished arrangement.

9 Left-side view of finished arrangement. Notice how the flowers are slanting forward.

ARRANGING STEPS

Before actually arranging, check where to put the display and make sure you work at the same eye level. Next, position the container so its front faces you. Fill it with water to 4/5 before you start. Refer to the pictures of materials for the length of each stem, but take advantage of the natural shapes of the materials rather than adjusting them to fit the examples shown in this book.

11 on page 1

Container:

Diam 7 cm × H 11 cm (2¾″ × 4½″)

42 cm (16¼″)

Materials:
Ivy (A)
Croton (B)
Orange flare cosmos (C)

1 Position ivy, hanging from the left side of container through handle.

2 Put 2 vines slanting left using natural shape.

3 Put croton starting at point of first ivy, slanting right.

4 Fill with cosmos so they spread naturally.

3 on page 7

Containers:

Diam 7 cm × H 13 cm (2¼″ × 5″)

66 cm (25¾″)

Materials:
Desert candle (A)
Myriocladus (B)

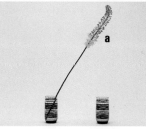

1 Putting cut end of desert candle against the inside of the vase, slant right.

2 Place (b) so that the top end touches (a).

3 Now (a) and (b) are supporting each other.

4 Cross myriocladus widely and add to (a).

5 Add remaining myriocladus to the right container, crossing stems.

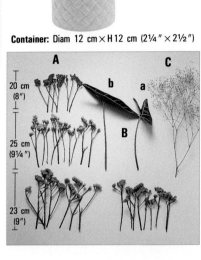

Materials: Statice (**A**)
Alocasia (**B**)
Baby's breath (**C**)

Container: Diam 12 cm × H 12 cm (2¼″ × 2½″)

A
b
a
C
20 cm (8″)
25 cm (9¼″)
23 cm (9″)
B

1 Bunch statice and put into vase, so florets face right and forward.

2 Insert alocasia (**a**), so leaf faces forward and left.

3 In front of (**a**), insert leaf (**b**) facing forward, tip pointing right.

4 Secure stem of alocasia (**b**).

5 Insert baby's breath in a round shape.

6 Right-side view of finished arrangement.

Container:

Hexagon of Diam 11 cm × H 9 cm
(4½″ × 3½″)

Materials:
Calla lily (**A**)
Lobster claw (**B**)
Stenophyllum (**C**)
Others:
Kenzan
(needlepoint holder)
Small vessel

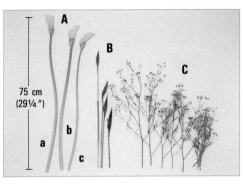

A
B
C
75 cm (29¼″)
a
b
c

1 Place a small vessel in container. Line with *kenzan*. Stand calla lily (**a**).

2 Add (**b**) and (**C**) to both sides, to form a fan shape.

3 Put stenophyllum in good proportion around base of calla lilies.

4 Add lobster claw to both sides of calla lily (**b**).

5 Rear view of finished arrangement.

6 Left-side view of finished arrangement.

Materials:
Japanese bead (**A**)
Gerbera daisy (**B**)
Delta maidenhair fern (**C**)

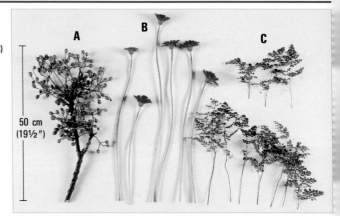

50 cm
(19½″)

Container:

W 35 cm × H 15 cm (13¾″ × 5¾″)

Rest at the rim
of the container.

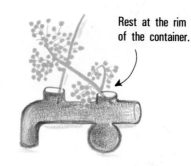

1 Position Japanese bead in right side opening, featuring its natural shape.

2 Place longest stemmed gerbera in left opening, slanting right.

3 Place another gerbera in left opening, slanting right. Place two gerberas in right opening, slightly inclining left.

4 Stand gerbera upright at back of right side opening. Insert shorter gerbera facing forward.

5 Insert delta maidenhair fern to cover front, right and back of left side flowers.

6 Finished arrangement. Notice overall balance.

7 Rear-view of finished arrangement.

8 Right-side view of finished arrangement.

9 Left-side view of finished arrangement. Notice angles of gerbera daisies.

8 on page 10

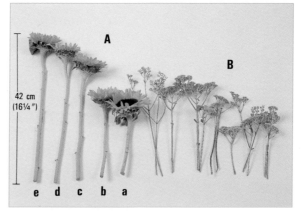

Container:

W 11 cm × D 11 cm × H 27 cm
(4½″ × 4½″ × 10½″)

42 cm
(16¼″)

A

B

e d c b a

Materials:
Sunflower (**A**)
Patrinia scabiosafolia (**B**)

1 Position sunflower (**a**) so that 2/3 of the flower head appear on right. Position (**b**) on left slanting low.

2 Stand (**c**) with flower facing right.

3 Position (**d**), aligning stem with (**c**). Add (**e**) so two flowers lean against each other.

4 Put patrinia scabiosafolia, to cover rim of vase and to cascade left.

5 Rear view of finished arrangement. Notice directions of flower heads.

6 Right-side view of finished arrangement.

7 Left-side view of finished arrangement. Notice patrinia scabiosafolia faces this side.

Position so that flower faces upward.

Strip the leaves from sunflower stems as they wilt easily.

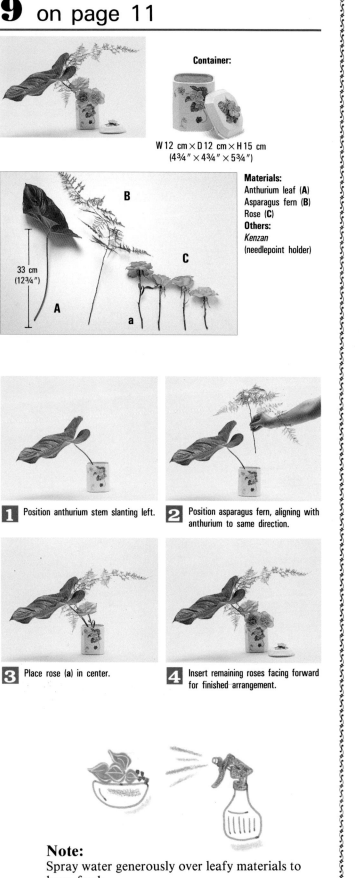

Container:

W 12 cm × D 12 cm × H 15 cm
(4¾" × 4¾" × 5¾")

Materials:
Anthurium leaf (**A**)
Asparagus fern (**B**)
Rose (**C**)
Others:
Kenzan
(needlepoint holder)

33 cm
(12¾")

B

C

A

a

1 Position anthurium stem slanting left.

2 Position asparagus fern, aligning with anthurium to same direction.

3 Place rose (a) in center.

4 Insert remaining roses facing forward for finished arrangement.

Note:
Spray water generously over leafy materials to keep fresh.

Container:

H 33 cm (12¾"),
with Diam 2 cm (¾") opening

Materials:
Caladium (**A**)
Ageratum (**B**)
Rose (**C**)

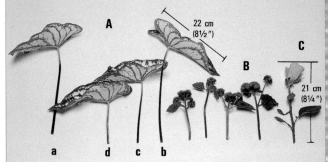

A

22 cm
(8½")

B

C

21 cm
(8¼")

a   d   c   b

1 Take caladium (**a**) and (**b**), cross the edges at rim of vase, and secure so that leaves face both sides.

2 Position (**c**) and (**d**) at center, inclining right and partly overlapping with each other.

3 Center rose, facing forward.

4 Fill with ageratum sprigs to cover the lower stem of rose.

5 Rear-view of finished arrangement.

6 Right-side view of finished arrangement.

10 on page 11

Materials: Hosta (**A**)
Kaffir lily (**B**)
Others: *Kenzan* (needlepoint holder)
Kansui-seki (white Japanese marble)

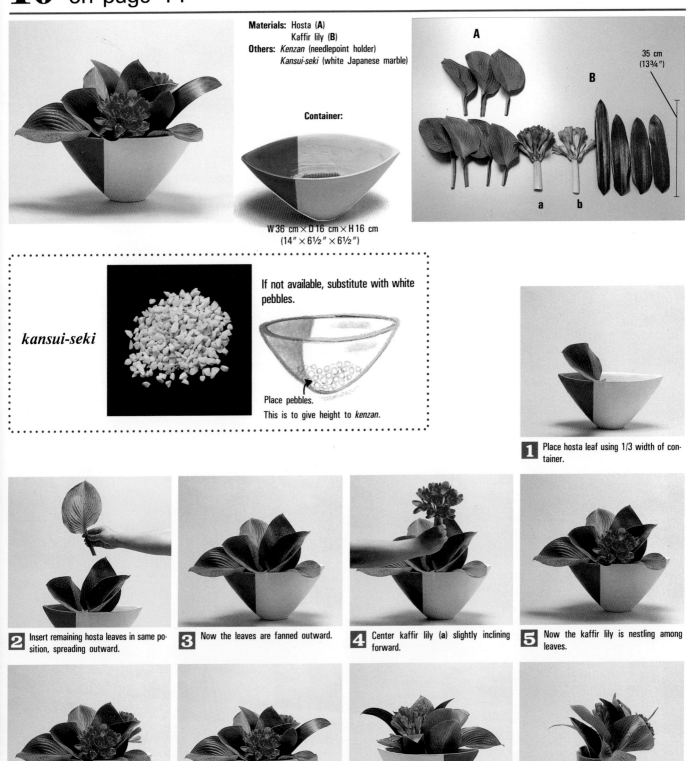

Container:

W 36 cm × D 16 cm × H 16 cm
(14″ × 6½″ × 6½″)

A

B

35 cm
(13¾″)

a   b

kansui-seki

If not available, substitute with white pebbles.

Place pebbles.
This is to give height to *kenzan*.

1 Place hosta leaf using 1/3 width of container.

2 Insert remaining hosta leaves in same position, spreading outward.

3 Now the leaves are fanned outward.

4 Center kaffir lily (**a**) slightly inclining forward.

5 Now the kaffir lily is nestling among leaves.

6 Insert kaffir lily (**b**) behind the leaves, to peek at right.

7 Finish with kaffir lily foliage.

8 Rear view of finished arrangement. Notice natural curvy lines of foliage.

9 Left-side view of finished arrangement. Notice flower heads facing forward.

Container:

Diam 9 cm × H 9 cm
(3½″ × 3½″)

Materials: Cornflower (**A**), Gerbera daisy (**B**), Miniature rose (**C**)
Others: *Kenzan* (needlepoint holder)

Note:
When displaying the arrangement, keep it out of the direct rays of the sun.

1 Place cornflower (**a**), in bottom left of container slanting toward front left.

2 Position (**b**) slightly inclining forward, with its head facing right.

3 Two stems are fanned out from a single point in *kenzan*

4 Center gerbera (**c**), facing forward. Add (**d**) behind (**b**), with its head a little lower.

5 Place miniature rose between (**a**) and (**c**), facing left and slightly forward.

6 Add remaining miniature roses to middle and back of container.

7 Rear view of finished arrangement. Notice directions of each flower.

8 Right-side view of finished arrangement.

9 Left-side view of finished arrangement.

15 on page 14

Container:

Diam 16 cm × H 13 cm
(6½″ × 5″)

Materials:
Palm (**A**)
Dracaena (**B**)
Peony (**C**)
Others:
Kenzan
(needlepoint holder)

65 cm
(25¼″)

A **B** **C**

b a

1 Center peony (**a**), facing slightly forward.

2 Position peony (**b**) behind (**a**), slightly inclining forward and left.

3 Set dracaena sprigs to spread to both sides.

4 Center palm so that it shows a wind-blown look.

30 on page 23

Container:

W 12 cm × D 7.5 cm × H 12 cm
(4¾″ × 3″ × 4¾″)

Materials:
Wisteria (**A**)
Hydrangea macrophylla normalis (**B**)
Others:
Kenzan
(needlepoint holder)

A

67 cm
(26¼″)

B

23 cm
(9″)

a b

1 Place wisteria (**a**) in left end of container, slanting toward front left to show the best of curvy line.

2 Position (**b**) almost horizontally extending toward front right.

3 Center hydrangea facing forward.

4 Right-side view of finished arrangement. Notice how hydrangea slants forward.

83

18 on page 15

Materials: Anthurium (**A**), Lady's mantle (**B**), Blazing-star (**C**)
Others: *Kenzan* (needlepoint holder), Small glass bowl

Container:

Hexagon of Diam 14 cm × H 10 cm
(5½" × 4")

32 cm
(12½")

Place *kenzan* in a small glass bowl before setting in the jewelry box.

Jewelry box

Kenzan

Glass bowl

1 Place blazing star (**a**) and (**c**) to face right and forward, resting stems on rim of container.

2 Add remaining blazing star in same manner.

3 Place anthurim slanting left, almost horizontally.

4 Add lady's mantle to lean over blazing star.

5 Rear view of finished arrangement.

6 Right-side view of finished arrangement. Notice blazing star and lady's mantle facing this side.

7 Left-side view of finished arrangement.

22 on page 18

Container:

Diam 14 cm × H 14.5 cm
(5½" × 5⅝")

Materials: Cosmos (**A**), Baby's breath (**B**), Sprengeri (**C**), Rice flower (**D**)
Others: *Kenzan* (needlepoint holder)

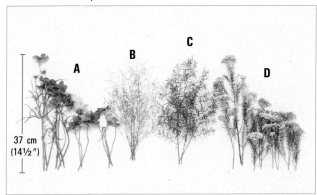

37 cm
(14½")

1 Place rice flower extending toward both sides, with left hand side shorter than right.

2 Add more rice flower to give volume to center.

3 Insert cosmoses to center, slanting left and right to balance with rice flower.

4 Add shorter stems of cosmos to front, slanting low.

5 Insert sprengeri sprigs into middle of display, to extend to both sides.

6 Insert baby's breath into middle extending to all directions to give fullness.

7 Rear view of finished arrangement.

8 Right-side view of finished arrangement. The whole arrangement looks round.

9 Left-side view of finished arrangement.

Materials: Ageratum (**A**)
Japanese beauty berry (**B**)
Feather cockscomb (**C**)

26 cm
(10¼ ")

Container: W 22 cm × H 23 cm (8½" × 9")
with Diam 6 cm (2¼ ") opening

1 Put Japanese beauty berry at an angle, extending from right rim of vase, showing natural curves.

2 From left rim of vase, extend another branch of Japanese beauty berry toward right.

3 Center feather cockscomb, facing forward.

4 Insert ageratum into front of vase to hide lower stems.

5 Rear view of finished arrangement.

6 Right-side view of finished arrangement. Notice flowers are slanting forward.

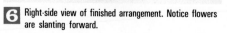

31 on page 24

Materials: Japanese banana plant (**A**)
Double-flowering cherry blossom (**B**)
Others: *Kenzan* (needlepoint holder)

75 cm
(29¼″)

a   **b**

When using a thick branch, slit the edge in a cross so as to absorb water well.

Container:
W 30 cm × D 9 cm × H 16 cm
(11¾″ × 3½″ × 6½″)

1 Position double-flowering cherry (**a**) in left side of *kenzan*, facing slightly forward.

2 Add (**b**) to the same point, slightly slanting right.

3 Place Japanese banana plant, aligning with (**b**).

4 Secure leaf to stand rigid. Check if it is extending along (**b**).

5 Stand another Japanese banana plant at front, using it as a plane.

6 Add shortest cherry twig to center front, slanting toward your left shoulder.

7 Rear view of finished arrangement.

8 Right-side view of finished arrangement. Notice angles of cherry and leaves.

9 Left-side view of finished arrangement.

Container:

Diam 15 cm × H 32 cm
(5¾″ × 12½″)

Materials: Hosta (**A**), Peruvian lily (**B**), Smilax (**C**)

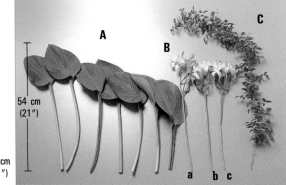

54 cm
(21″)

Arrange leaves intersecting the stems in
the vase.

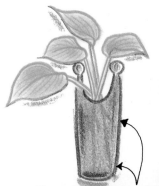

Edges are touching the inner wall for
stability.

1 Place hosta in vase so its cut
edge touches inside wall, and its
leaf slants forward.

2 Place more leaves to left, right
and back, intersecting stems in
vase.

3 Add remaining leaves so their tips
face every direction.

4 Center Peruvian lily (**a**) slanting
forward.

5 Check to see if Peruvian lily has
same height as longest hosta
leaf.

6 Position another Peruvian lily (**b**)
at back left of (**a**).

7 Add (**c**) to back of (**a**).

8 Add smilax to left rim, climbing
up and around flowers, then cascading to right.

9 Finished arrangement.

10 Left-side view of finished
arrangement. Notice how smilax
vine is winding around flowers.

33 on page 26

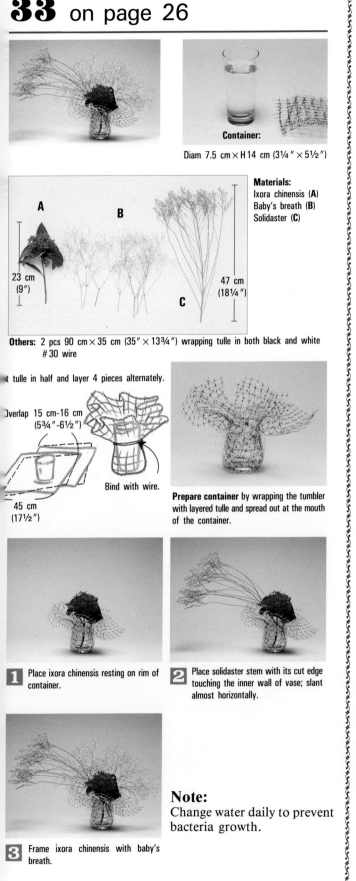

Container:
Diam 7.5 cm × H 14 cm (3¼″ × 5½″)

Materials:
Ixora chinensis (**A**)
Baby's breath (**B**)
Solidaster (**C**)

A
B
23 cm (9″)
47 cm (18¼″)
C

Others: 2 pcs 90 cm × 35 cm (35″ × 13¾″) wrapping tulle in both black and white
#30 wire

t tulle in half and layer 4 pieces alternately.

Overlap 15 cm-16 cm (5¾″-6½″)
Bind with wire.
45 cm (17½″)

Prepare container by wrapping the tumbler with layered tulle and spread out at the mouth of the container.

1 Place ixora chinensis resting on rim of container.

2 Place solidaster stem with its cut edge touching the inner wall of vase; slant almost horizontally.

3 Frame ixora chinensis with baby's breath.

Note:
Change water daily to prevent bacteria growth.

35 on page 27

Container:

W 38 cm × D 5 cm × H 10 cm
(14¾″ × 2″ × 4″)

Materials:
Dianthus (**A**)
Camellia (**B**)
Others:
2 *kenzan*
(needlepoint holder)

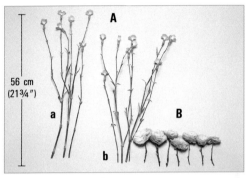

A
56 cm (21¾″)
a
b
B

1 Place dianthuses (**a**) at middle left of container, showing natural lines. Be sure to place stem ends at a single point.

2 Place dianthuses (**b**) at middle right, in a triangular shape.

3 Add camellias to bottom, so they look nestled together.

4 Right-side view of finished arrangement.

Materials: Japanese maholia (**A**), Chrysanthemum (**B**), Speedwell (**C**), Thalictrum (**D**)
Others: *Kenzan* (needlepoint holder)

Container:
W 22 cm × D 15 cm × H 10 cm
(8½″ × 5¾″ × 4″)

A
38 cm (14¾″)
B
a b c d e

58 cm (22½″)
C
D

1 Position Japanese maholia (**a**) at middle left, slanting toward your left shoulder.

2 Place (**b**) in middle right, slanting low.

3 Stand chrysanthemum (**e**) upright in middle.

4 Add chrysanthemums (**c**) and (**d**) on both sides of (**e**), slanting forward.

5 Take a speedwell stem and place in front right of (**e**), showing natural flowing line.

6 Add remaining speedwells to back, front and right.

7 Using short-stemmed speedwells, fill the front of chrysanthemums, so they bow to you.

8 Insert feather columbine in middle left.

9 Rear view of finished arrangement. Check to see how speedwells flow.

10 Right-side view of finished arrangement.

11 Left-side view of finished arrangement.

36 on page 27

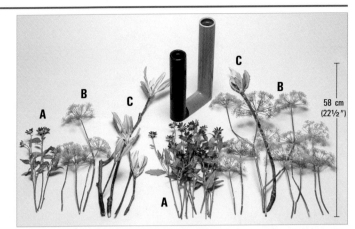

Materials: China aster (**A**)
Fennel (**B**)
Magnolia hypoleuca (**C**)

Container: W 19 cm × H 31 cm (7½″ × 12″), with 6 cm (2¼″) openings

58 cm
(22½″)

Note:
Cut branches at 45° angle. Oblique cut edges can be easily pushed into *kenzan* (needlepoint holder).

1 Place 2 branches of magnolia in both openings, crossing at middle right and extending forward.

2 Place short branches of magnolia in left opening, slanting each forward left and back.

3 Cover rim of vase with fennel, facing toward middle of display.

4 Insert fennel into right opening, extending left.

5 Insert China asters into left opening, slanting forward.

6 Put remaining China asters into left opening in same manner.

7 Rear view of finished arrangement.

8 Right-side view of same arrangement. Notice magnolia is protruding.

9 Left-side view of finished arrangement.

Container:

W 46 cm × D 8.5 cm × H 8 cm
(18″ × 3¼″ × 3⅛″)

78 cm
(30½″)

A

B

C

a b c

Materials: Macleaya cordata (**A**), Delphinium (**B**), Solidaster (**C**)
Others: 2 *kenzan* (needlepoint holder)

1 Position Macleaya cordata in middle left of container, slanting naturally to right.

2 Place another leaf in front, flowing almost palarell but slightly forward.

3 Place shortest leaf in same point, slanting left.

4 Stand delphinium (**c**) in middle of leaves.

5 Stand delphinium (**b**) at left of (**a**).

6 Place (**a**) between (**b**) and (**c**), slanting slightly forward.

7 Group solidasters and place in front of delphiniums.

8 Add remaining solidasters in front of foliage.

9 Rear view of finished arrangement.

10 Right-side view of finished arrangement. Notice positions of delphiniums.

11 Left-side view of finished arrangement.

Note: Keep Container Clean!
Thoroughly wash the container before using. Remove any stain or dust because slimy inner wall causes bacteria.

38 on page 28

Materials: African lily (**A**)
Wax tree (**B**)
Lace flower (**C**)
Others: 2 *kenzan*
(needlepoint holder)

65 cm
(25¼ ")

Container:

W 24 cm × D 9 cm × H 11 cm
(9¼ " × 3½ " × 4½ ")

Fill with water so that the cut edges of materials
are completely covered.

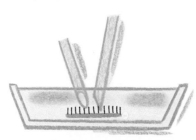

1 Position African lily (**a**) in left edge of *kenzan*, slanting right and slightly forward.

2 Place (**b**) in same point as (**a**), almost upright. Place (**c**) in right edge of *kenzan* at an angle so that stems cross as shown.

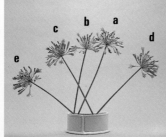

3 Place (**d**) in same point as (**c**), slanting front right. Add (**e**) to base of (**a**) also at a slant, so flowers fan out.

4 Set wax tree on left, facing forward.

5 Fill mouth of container with wax tree.

6 Finish with lace flower sprigs setting a little higher than foliage.

7 Rear view of finished arrangement. Notice African lilies are fanned out.

8 Right-side view of finished arrangement.

9 Left-side view of finished arrangement. The whole arrangement are slanting front.

Materials: Allium schubertii (**A**)
Glory lily (**B**)
Smilax (**C**)

Container:

W 27.5 cm × D 6 cm × H 15 cm
(10¾″ × 2¼″ × 5¾″)

58 cm
(22½″)

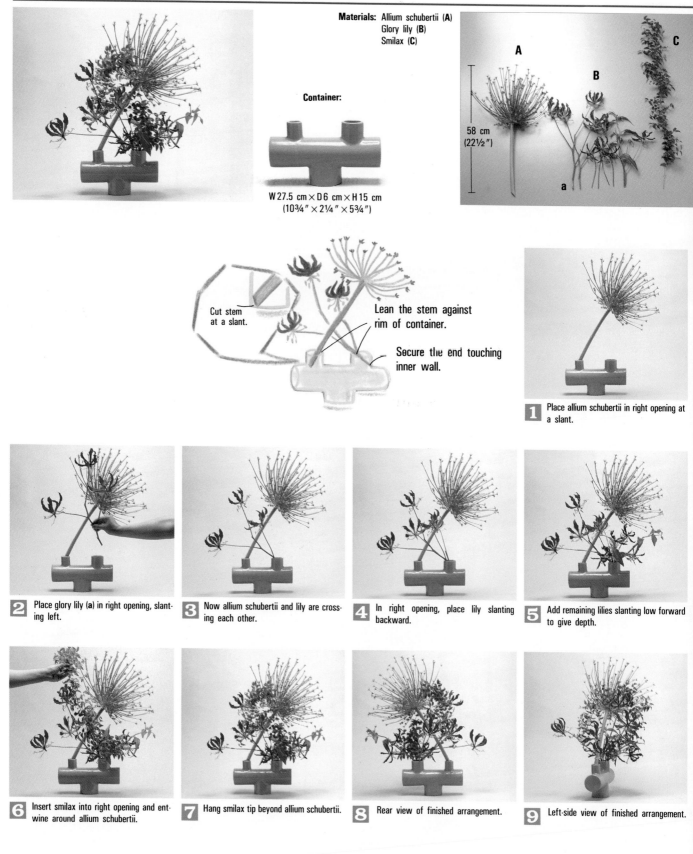

Cut stem
at a slant.

Lean the stem against
rim of container.

Secure the end touching
inner wall.

1 Place allium schubertii in right opening at a slant.

2 Place glory lily (**a**) in right opening, slanting left.

3 Now allium schubertii and lily are crossing each other.

4 In right opening, place lily slanting backward.

5 Add remaining lilies slanting low forward to give depth.

6 Insert smilax into right opening and entwine around allium schubertii.

7 Hang smilax tip beyond allium schubertii.

8 Rear view of finished arrangement.

9 Left-side view of finished arrangement.

40 on page 29

Materials: Satsuma mock orangre (**A**)
Kaffir lily (**B**)

Container:
Diam 7 cm × H 37 cm
(2¾″ × 14½″)

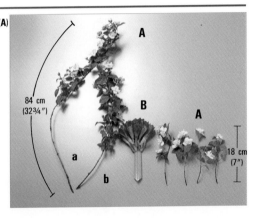

84 cm
(32¾″)

A

B

A

18 cm
(7″)

a

b

Note:
When displaying the arrangement, avoid where the cool air is blown from air conditioner as it will cause dryness.

1 Place satsuma mock orangre (**a**) in right side of vase, hanging naturally right.

2 In left side of vase, place (**b**), hanging left.

3 Now branches are hanging both ways showing gentle curves.

4 Place kaffir lily facing forward.

5 Now mouth of vase is filled with kaffir lily.

6 Fill out with remaining twigs, by inserting into front and back.

7 Rear view of finished arrangement.

8 Right-side view of finished arrangement. Notice the whole arrangement is slanting forward.

9 Left-side view of finished arrangement.

Containers:

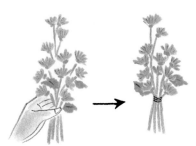

Diam 7.5 cm × H 14 cm (3″ × 5½″)

Bind several stems together.

Top

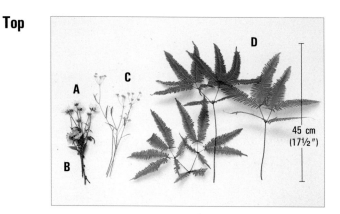

45 cm
(17½″)

Materials: Small chrysanthemum (**A**), Spraymum (**B**), Stenophyllum (**C**), Fern (**D**)
Others: #30 wire

1 Bind spray mums and small chrysanthemums with wire and put in container. Add stenophyllum.

2 Insert fern slanting forward. Add another to back.

Middle

42 cm
(16¼″)

Materials: Small chrysanthemum (**A**), Stenophyllum (**B**), Spraymum (**C**), Fern (**D**)
Others: #30 wire

1 Put spray mums and small chrysanthemums so flowers stick forward. Add stenophyllum higher at back left.

2 Insert fern fronds so as to hang over chrysanthemums.

Bottom

52 cm
(20¼″)

Materials: Stenophyllum (**A**), Small chrysanthemum (**B**), Fern (**C**)
Others: #30 wire

1 Put spray mums and small chrysanthemums so flowers stick forward. Add stenophyllum slanting right.

2 Finish with fern flowing from left to right.

42 on page 31

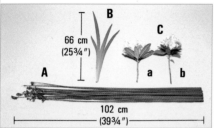

Container:
Diam 12 cm × H 23 cm
(4¾″ × 9″)

Materials: Japanese bulrush (**A**), Iris leaf (**B**), Alpine rose (**C**)
Others: *Kenzan* (needlepoint holder)

1 Holding 17 stalks of Japanese bulrush together, stand upright in the middle.

2 Insert alpine rose (**a**) into center front, sticking forward.

3 Add (**b**) to left, in the same height.

4 Bend center 2 stalks down to height of flowers. Finish with iris leaves adding to opposite side.

43 on page 31

Container:
W 18 cm × D 12 cm × H 23 cm
(7″ × 4¾″ × 9″)

Materials: Selloum (**A**), Baby's breath (**B**), Japanese bulrush (**C**)

1 Holding 30 stalks of Japanese bulrush together, slant right securing ends at inside of vase.

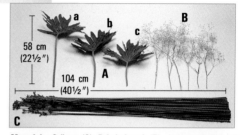

2 Add selloum (**a**) slanting lower.

3 Place (**b**) in middle, with tip pointing downward.

4 Insert (**c**) behind (**b**), and add baby's breath to give fullness.

Materials: Japanese banana plant (**A**)
Allium giganteum (**B**)
Asparagus fern (**C**)
Blue fantasy (**D**)
Others: *Kenzan* (needlepoint holder)
Pebbles

88 cm
(34¼")

Container:

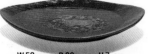

W 50 cm × D 38 cm × H 7 cm
(19½" × 14¾" × 2¾")

Position *kenzan* and pebbles in center of *suiban* (shallow container).

Note:
When displaying your arrangement, avoid places near open window. Even a soft breeze could dry the flowers.

1 Stand allium giganteum (**a**) in center.

2 Place Japanese banana plant right next to (**a**) at a slant.

3 Place another leaf on left, slanting lower.

4 Stand (**b**) in front of (**a**).

5 Add asparagus fern at back, as high as allium (**b**).

6 Place remaining asparagus fern at front, to neaten base part and to hide *kenzan*.

7 Finish with blue fantasy added to back of (**a**), in same height with (**b**).

8 Rear view of finished arrangement.

9 Left-side view of finished arrangement. Take notice that all are arranged in a straight line.

48 on page 35

Materials: Satsuma mock orangre (**A**)
Hosta (**B**)
Peruvian lily (**C**)
Prairie gentian (**D**)
Others: #30 wire

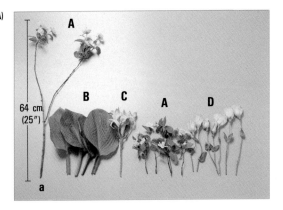

Container: Diam 10 cm × H 30 cm
(4″ × 11¾″)

Wipe leaves clean.   Layer 4 leaves and bind with wire.

Trim satsuma mock orangre. Save short twigs to use later for the base of arrangement.

1 Place satsuma mock orangre (**a**) at a slant.

2 Place bound hosta so as to extend toward left.

3 Cover rim of vase with cut-off twigs.

4 Insert Peruvian lily in right, slanting forward.

5 Finish with prairie gentian inserted in all sides of Peruvian lily.

6 Rear view of finished arrangement.

7 Right-side view of finished arrangement. Notice much attention was given to flowers at back.

49 on page 35

Materials: Beargrass (**A**)
Peony (**B**)
Candytuft (**C**)
Others: *Kenzan*
(needlepoint holder)
30 wire

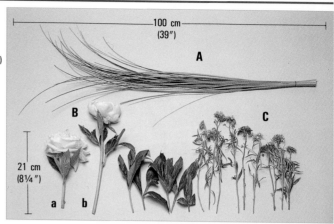

Container:

W 41 cm × D 23 cm × H 5.5 cm (16″ × 9″ × 2⅛″)

Place *kenzan* at front left of *suiban* (shallow container).

Be careful when beargrass since the blades are sharp.

1 Position peony (**a**) slanting toward you.

2 Hide *kenzan* with peony leaves.

3 Place peony (**b**) behind (**a**), slanting right and up at 45°.

4 Add candytufts, varying the lengths and directions extending from behind (**b**).

5 Bind beargrass with wire and shape it to droop in all directions; stand it behind (**a**).

6 Rear view of finished arrangement.

7 Left-side view of finished arrangement. Notice how flowers are slanted.

After wiring beargrass, stroke blades through your hand to create a "fountain" effect.

50 on page 36

Materials: Billberry (**A**)
　　　　　　Ageratum (**B**)
　　　　　　Smokegrass (**C**)
Others: *Kenzan* (needlepoint holder)
　　　　　　Small bowl

51 cm
(20")

58 cm
(22½")

23 cm
(9")

A

B

C

Container:

W 18.5 cm × D 9.5 cm × H 9 cm
(7¼" × 3¾" × 3½")

alcohol

To keep smokegrass fresh, cut under water and dip into alcohol.

1 Place billberry in middle right of container.

2 Check to see if the most interesting natural line of the billberry branch is showing.

3 Add ageratum to base of billberry, facing toward.

4 Now ageratum is secured.

5 Stand smokegrass at base of billberry slanting forward and left.

6 Finished arrangement.

7 Rear view of finished arrangement.

8 Right-side view of finished arrangement. Notice ageratum is facing forward.

52 on page 38

Materials: Arrowwood (**A**), Peony (**B**)
Others: 2 *kenzan* (needlepoint holder), 2 small vessels

Container:

W 42 cm × D 23 cm × H 25 cm
(16¼″ × 9″ × 9¾″)

Place 2 small vessels in the basket, lay *kenzan* in each.

1 Stand arrowwood upright on right side of handle.

2 On left side, place arrowwood low.

3 Place peony (**a**) at center right, slanting forward.

4 Add (**b**) in front of (**a**), slanting lower.

5 On left side of (**b**), place (**c**). Add (**d**) to left side, then (**e**) at back.

6 Place long-stemmed white peony so that it protrudes toward right.

7 Insert remaining white peonies, varying lengths.

8 Rear view of finished arrangement. Notice directions of flowers.

9 Right-side view of finished arrangement.

10 Left-side view of finished arrangement. Notice white peonies are protruding forward.

54 on page 39

Materials: Spiroea (**A**)
Balloonflower (**B**)

57 cm
(22¼")

A

B

a b

Container:
Diam 4 cm × H 33 cm
(1½" × 12¾")

1 Stand spirea rigidly upright from left rim of vase.

2 Place balloonflower (**a**) slanting forward and slightly right.

3 Insert remaining balloonflowers (**b**) around (**a**), slanting toward same direction.

4 Right-side view of finished arrangement. Notice how balloonflowers are slanting forward.

79 on page 57

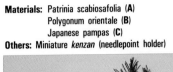

Materials: Patrinia scabiosafolia (**A**)
Polygonum orientale (**B**)
Japanese pampas (**C**)
Others: Miniature *kenzan* (needlepoint holder)

75 cm
(29¼")

A B C

Container:
Diam 15 cm × H 27 cm
(5¾" × 10½")

1 Position polygonum orientale at center of container inserting in front of handle, slightly facing forward.

2 Fill out with patrinia scabiosafolia, standing upright from front.

3 Finish with Japanese pampas of varied lengths, to droop over polygonum orientale.

4 Right-side view of finished arrangement. Notice most flowers are slanting slightly forward.

Container: W 27 cm × D 8 cm × H 5 cm
(10½″ × 3⅛″ × 2″)

Position *kenzan* on the left side of the container.

Left Arrangement

48 cm
(18¾″)

Materials:
Mountain laurel
Others:
Kenzan
(needlepoint holder)

1 Place mountain laurel (**a**) at a slant on left side of container.

2 Stand (**b**) upright on left of (**a**). Place (**c**) at a slant on very left.

3 Add (**d**) and (**e**) slanting forward, positioning at a single point.

4 Rear view of finished arrangement.

5 Right-side view of finished arrangement. Notice direction of shorter stems.

6 Left-side view of finished arrangement.

Right Arrangement

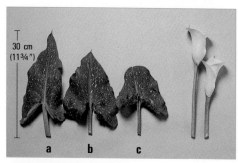

30 cm
(11¾″)

Materials: Calla lily
Others: *Kenzan* (needlepoint holder)

1 Place calla lily leaf (**a**) at a slant in left side of container.

2 Add leaf (**b**) to right of (**a**), tip pointing backward. Add (**c**) in front, slanting low.

3 Secure calla lilies among leaves, slanting one forward, and the other toward your right shoulder.

66 on page 49

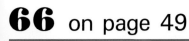

Materials: *Janome* pine (**A**)
Japanese winterberry (**B**)
Small chrysanthemum (**C**)

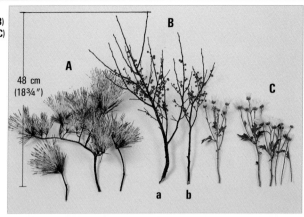

48 cm
(18¾")

Container:

Diam 9 cm × H 23 cm
(3½" × 9")

Note: GREEN AND RED FOR THE NEW YEAR'S?
There is a reason why foliage such as pine or bamboo and red flowers or berries are used in the festive arrangements. Green color is said to stand for an eternal life, red color for the will to live, and gold color for richness.

1 Position Japanese winterberry (**a**) almost horizontally to left of container showing it to its best advantage.

2 Place (**b**) to right of container slanting back right.

3 Now branches are extending to both sides to create a dramatic mood.

4 Insert *janome* pine branches, one in same direction as (**b**), others slanting forward to cover rim of vase.

5 Insert small chrysanthemum stems in center, slanting forward.

6 Left-side view of finished arrangement. Notice *janome* pine are slanting low.

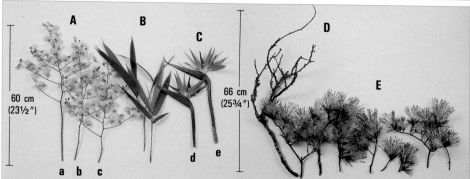

Materials: Oncidium (**A**), Bamboo (**B**), Bird-of-paradise (**C**), Lichened plum (**D**), Janome pine (**E**)
Others: Red/white and silver/gold *mizuhiki* (paper cord), *Kenzan* (needlepoint holder), #30 wire

Container:

W 41 cm × D 23 cm × H 5 cm (16″ × 9″ × 2″)

Place *kenzan* at left front of container.

30 cm (11¾″)
3 pcs   9 pcs
50 cm (19½″)
mizuhiki
2.5 cm (1″)
Wind twice and secure several points with wire.

1 Center lichened plum slanting back right, checking its shape.

2 Place *janome* pine on left, also slanting backward.

3 Add another pine twig in front, slanting toward your left shoulder.

4 Add another twig leaning forward so all appear to extend from a single point.

5 Add more twigs to give width and fullness.

6 Stand bird-of-paradise (**e**) in middle left, facing left.

7 Insert (**d**) in front of plum, slanting forward and right, tip facing same direction.

8 Insert bamboo stems behind (**e**), and between (**d**) and (**e**), a little higher than pine.

9 Place oncidium (**a**) at back of *kenzan*, (**b**) and (**c**) in front, to give volume.

10 Attach shaped *mizuhiki* to lichened branch using wire. Check overall balance.

11 Rear view of finished arrangement. Check back side of *mizuhiki* and how oncidium is flowing.

12 Left-side view of finished arrangement.

67 on page 50

Materials: Pine (**A**), Rose (**B**), Blue fantasy (**C**)
Others: *Kenzan* (needlepoint holder)

Container:

W 55 cm × D 11 cm × H 8 cm (21½″ × 4½″ × 3⅛″)

Place *kenzan* at right side of container.

Remove leaves from the stems because leaves under water will spoil the clean water.

1 Secure pine on *kenzan*, slanting almost horizontally toward front left.

2 Center rose (**a**) inclining slightly toward your right shoulder.

3 Now pine and rose are extending in both directions balancing one another.

4 On both sides of (**a**), place (**b**) and (**c**) slanting forward.

5 Fill out with blue fantasy.

6 Rear view of finished arrangement. Notice pine branch is extending naturally low.

7 Right-side view of finished arrangement.

Be sure to position rose so its flower head faces upward.

68 on page 51

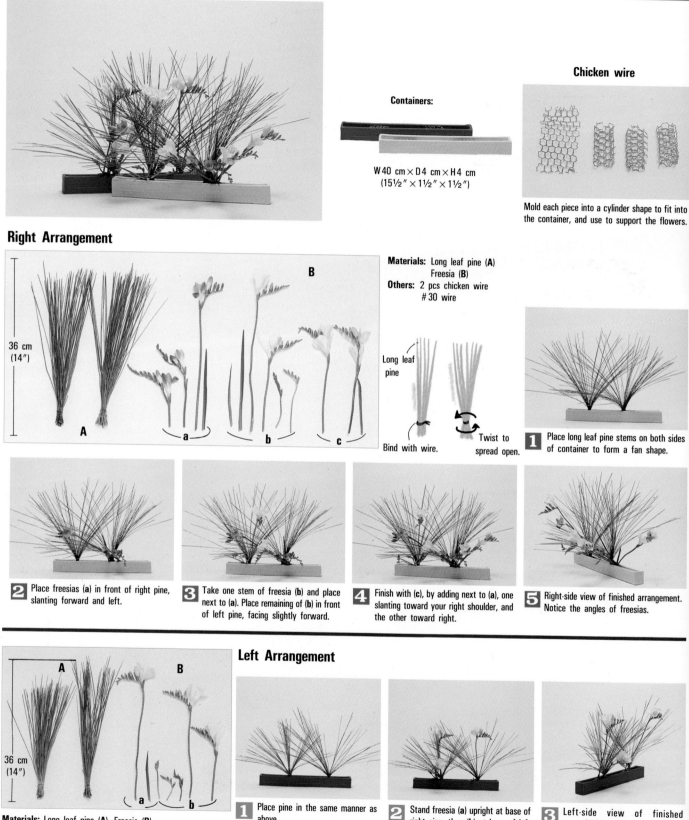

Chicken wire

Mold each piece into a cylinder shape to fit into the container, and use to support the flowers.

Containers:

W 40 cm × D 4 cm × H 4 cm
(15½″ × 1½″ × 1½″)

Right Arrangement

Materials: Long leaf pine (**A**)
Freesia (**B**)
Others: 2 pcs chicken wire
30 wire

36 cm
(14″)

A　　**a**　　**b**　　**c**　　**B**

Long leaf pine

Bind with wire.　Twist to spread open.

1 Place long leaf pine stems on both sides of container to form a fan shape.

2 Place freesias (**a**) in front of right pine, slanting forward and left.

3 Take one stem of freesia (**b**) and place next to (**a**). Place remaining of (**b**) in front of left pine, facing slightly forward.

4 Finish with (**c**), by adding next to (**a**), one slanting toward your right shoulder, and the other toward right.

5 Right-side view of finished arrangement. Notice the angles of freesias.

Left Arrangement

A　**B**

36 cm
(14″)

a　**b**

Materials: Long leaf pine (**A**), Freesia (**B**)
Others: 2 pcs chicken wire, # 30 wire

1 Place pine in the same manner as above.

2 Stand freesia (**a**) upright at base of right pine, then (**b**) at base of left pine.

3 Left-side view of finished arrangement.

69 on page 51

Materials: Lichend plum blanch (**A**)
Long leaf pine (**B**)
Lobster claw (**C**)
Others: *Kenzan* (needlepoint holder)
Mizuhiki (paper cord)
#30 wire

Container:

W 8.5 cm × D 8.5 cm × H 13 cm
(3¼″ × 3¼″ × 5″)

63 cm
(24½″)

50 pcs *mizuhiki* in gold
46 pcs *mizuhiki* in silver
30 pcs *mizuhiki* in red
25 pcs *mizuhiki* in white

Using a short branch as a
core, wire all cords by binding 2-3 times.

8 cm
(3⅛″)

1 cm   2 cm   2 cm
(⅜″)   (¾″)   (¾″)

Spare branch

1 Bind base of pine needles with wire, and place so that
they spread softly.

2 Add bound cords right next to pine so they spread in the
same density.

3 Place lichened plum branch at front, slanting a little forward to show its freely extending line.

4 Finish by centering stems of lobster claw, slanting one
forward.

5 Rear view of finished arrangement. Check to see if pine
needles and *mizuhiki* are fanning in the same manner.

6 Right-side view of finished arrangement. Notice angles
of plum and lobster claw.

7 Left-side view of finished arrangement.

Containers:

W 28 cm × D 24.5 cm × H 15 cm
(11″ × 9½″ × 5¾″)

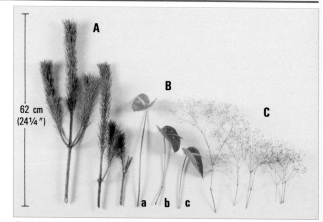

62 cm
(24¼″)

Materials: Young pine (**A**), Anthurium (**B**), Baby's breath (**C**)
Others: *Kenzan* (needlepoint holder)

1 Secure tallest pine in center, slanting toward your left shoulder.

2 Add remaining pine sprigs to front so that all stems extend from a single pint.

3 Place anthurium (**a**) at a slant, facing slightly forward.

4 Add (**b**) and (**c**) to front, parallel to each other and hiding rim of vase.

5 Insert baby's breath in middle to give softness.

6 Add another sprig of baby's breath at back to give depth.

7 Rear view of finished arrangement. Notice anthurium (**a**) is extending to side.

8 Left-side view of finished arrangement.

9 Notice that the whole arrangement is facing forward when viewed from right.

74 on page 55

Materials: Spirea (**A**)
Sweetflag (**B**)
Others: 2 *kenzan*
(needlepoint holder)

80 cm
(31¼")

The Right Side of Blade:

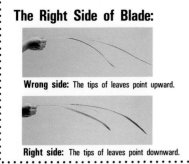

Wrong side: The tips of leaves point upward.

Right side: The tips of leaves point downward.

Direction of Flower:

Front

The direction of bud indicates to which side the flower opens.

Container:

W 41 cm × D 23 cm × H 5.5 cm (16" × 9" × 2⅛")

Position *kenzan*, one at front left corner and the other at middle right.

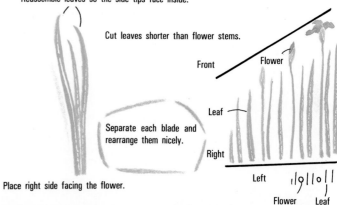

Reassemble leaves so the side tips face inside.

Cut leaves shorter than flower stems.

Front

Flower

Leaf

Separate each blade and rearrange them nicely.

Right

Place right side facing the flower.

Left

Flower   Leaf

1 Stand sweetflag (**a**) at left side, and (**b**) at right back.

2 Rearrange leaves and place in front of (**b**). Add more rearranged leaves to front, showing flower heads between leaves.

3 Rearrange leaves to add to (**a**), and place almost parallel to each other.

4 Place thin spirea sprigs to expand to sides.

5 Rear view of finished arrangement.

6 Left-side view of finished arrangement. Notice positions of (**a**) and (**b**) are creating depth.

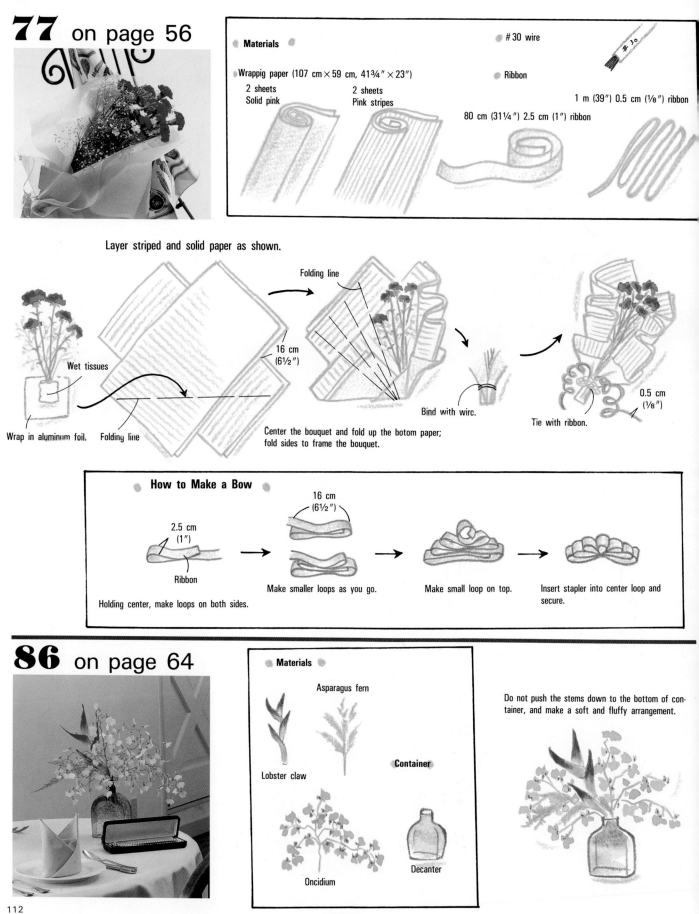

77 on page 56

Materials

Wrappig paper (107 cm × 59 cm, 41¾" × 23")

2 sheets
Solid pink

2 sheets
Pink stripes

#30 wire

Ribbon

1 m (39") 0.5 cm (⅛") ribbon

80 cm (31¼") 2.5 cm (1") ribbon

Layer striped and solid paper as shown.

Wet tissues

Wrap in aluminum foil.

Folding line

Folding line

16 cm
(6½")

Center the bouquet and fold up the botom paper;
fold sides to frame the bouquet.

Bind with wirc.

Tie with ribbon.

0.5 cm
(⅛")

How to Make a Bow

2.5 cm
(1")

Ribbon

Holding center, make loops on both sides.

16 cm
(6½")

Make smaller loops as you go.

Make small loop on top.

Insert stapler into center loop and secure.

86 on page 64

Materials

Asparagus fern

Lobster claw

Container

Oncidium

Decanter

Do not push the stems down to the bottom of container, and make a soft and fluffy arrangement.

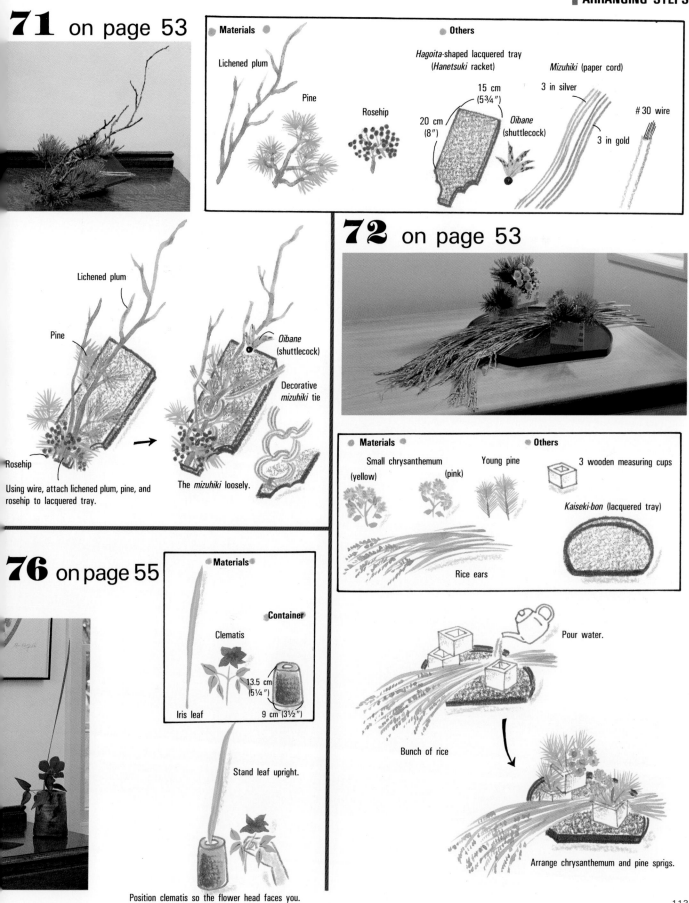

71 on page 53

Materials

Lichened plum

Pine

Rosehip

Others

Hagoita-shaped lacquered tray
(*Hanetsuki* racket)

15 cm
(5¾")

20 cm
(8")

Mizuhiki (paper cord)

3 in silver

Oibane
(shuttlecock)

3 in gold

30 wire

Lichened plum

Pine

Rosehip

Oibane
(shuttlecock)

Decorative
mizuhiki tie

The *mizuhiki* loosely.

Using wire, attach lichened plum, pine, and
rosehip to lacquered tray.

72 on page 53

Materials

Small chrysanthemum
(yellow)

(pink)

Young pine

Rice ears

Others

3 wooden measuring cups

Kaiseki-bon (lacquered tray)

Pour water.

Bunch of rice

Arrange chrysanthemum and pine sprigs.

76 on page 55

Materials

Container

Clematis

13.5 cm
(5¼")

Iris leaf

9 cm (3½")

Stand leaf upright.

Position clematis so the flower head faces you.

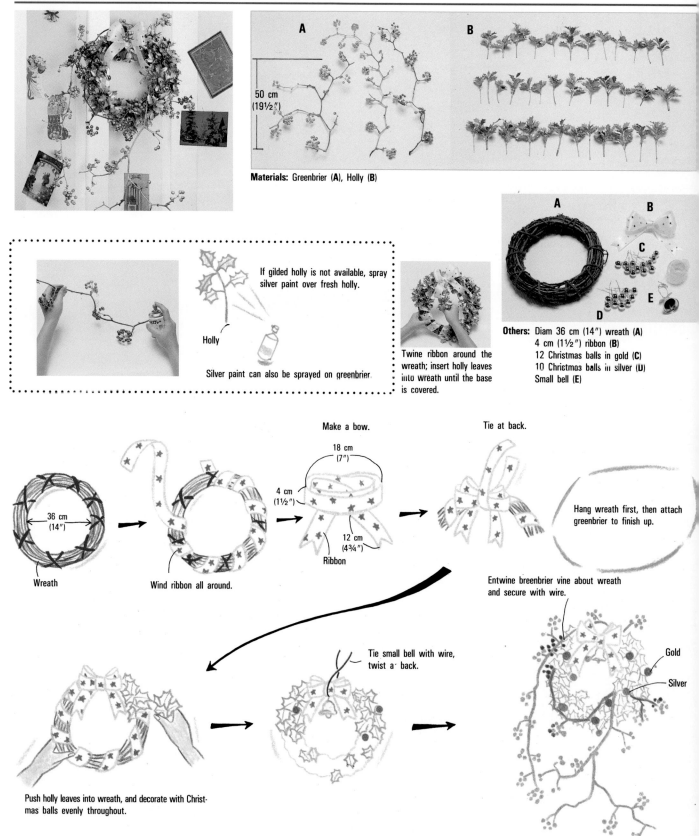

Materials: Greenbrier (**A**), Holly (**B**)

If gilded holly is not available, spray silver paint over silver paint over fresh holly.

Holly

Silver paint can also be sprayed on greenbrier.

Twine ribbon around the wreath; insert holly leaves into wreath until the base is covered.

Others: Diam 36 cm (14″) wreath (**A**)
4 cm (1½″) ribbon (**B**)
12 Christmas balls in gold (**C**)
10 Christmas balls in silver (**D**)
Small bell (**E**)

Make a bow.

Tie at back.

36 cm
(14″)

Wreath

Wind ribbon all around.

18 cm
(7″)

4 cm
(1½″)

12 cm
(4¾″)

Ribbon

Hang wreath first, then attach greenbrier to finish up.

Entwine breenbrier vine about wreath and secure with wire.

Push holly leaves into wreath, and decorate with Christmas balls evenly throughout.

Tie small bell with wire, twist at back.

Gold

Silver

82 on page 60

Materials: Japanese winterberry (**A**)
Poinsettia (**B**)
Others: Iridescent tinsel

55 cm
(21½")

Container:

W 22 cm × D 6 cm × H 22 cm
(8½" × 2¼" × 8½")

Iridescent tinsel

1 Stand Japanese winterberry (**b**) at center to show off its natural curves.

2 Place (**a**) at a slant, crossing stems with (**b**).

3 Insert (**c**) into right end of container, slanting almost horizontally. Stand (**d**) upright at left.

4 Insert poinsettia into left of container, with its head facing you.

5 Hang iridescent tinsel all over almost reaching bottom of container.

6 Left-side view of finished arrangement. Notice all branches are extending forward.

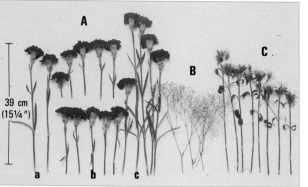

Materials: Carnation (**A**)
Baby's breath (**B**)
Dianthus (**C**)
Others: *Kenzan* (needlepoint holder)

39 cm
(15¼")

a   b   c

Container:

W 29 cm × D 9 cm × H 19 cm
(11¼" × 3½" × 7½")

Wrap *kenzan* (needlepoint holder) with tissue to
protect the surface of the glass container.

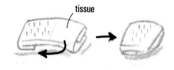

tissue

1 Place carnations (**a**) at center, slanting
right.

2 Fill mouth of container with carnations
(**b**) to form a low dome shape.

3 Stand carnations (**c**) at center, slightly inclining toward right.

4 Insert dianthus stems in middle to right
end of container.

5 Add baby's breath in middle to left of container.

6 Rear view of finished arrangement. Notice all carnations are positioned on left
half of whole display.

7 Right-side view of finished arrangement.

8 Left-side view of finished arrangement.
Check to see how baby's breath is
spreading.

84 on page 62

Materials: Amacrinum lily (**A**)
Curly fern (**B**)
Spider plant (**C**)
Others: Birthday card

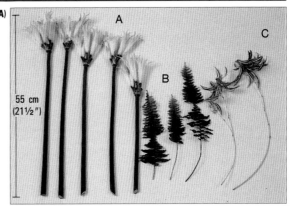

A

B

C

55 cm
(21½")

Container:

W 26 cm × D 5 cm × H 20 cm
(10¼" × 2" × 8")

Flower stems are cut at right angle.

1 Bundle amacrinum lilies and place in vase slanting toward your left shoulder.

2 Insert spider plant to hang over rim of vase, toward your right shoulder.

3 Now amacrinum lilies and spider plant are balancing each other.

4 Insert curly fern slanting left, almost horizontally.

5 Insert a card into stem base at an angle.

6 Front view of finished arrangement.

7 Rear view of finished arrangement.

8 Right-side view of finished arrangement.

9 Left-side view of finished arrangement.

Gold Arrangement   **Silver Arrangement**

Containers:

Diam 30 cm × H 5 cm (11¾″ × 2″)

Others: Candles (**A**)
Spray paint (**B**)
Angel-hair (**C**)

A
C
30 cm
(11¾″)
B

If gilded holly is not available, spray gold and silver paint on fresh holly.

Cut end of 3 cm-4 cm (1″-1½″) twig at a slant, and push into the bottom of candle.

Silver Arrangement
(Right)

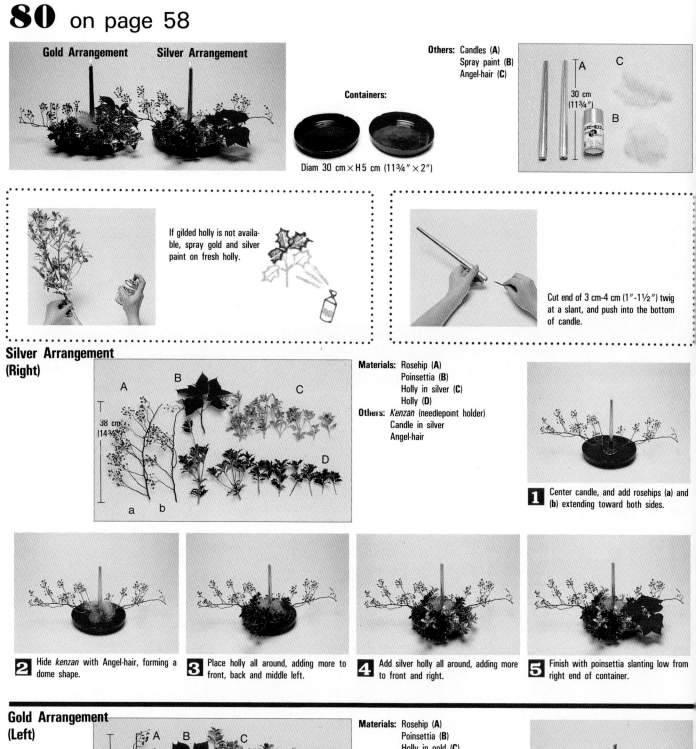

A   B   C
38 cm
(14¾″)
D
a   b

Materials: Rosehip (**A**)
Poinsettia (**B**)
Holly in silver (**C**)
Holly (**D**)
Others: *Kenzan* (needlepoint holder)
Candle in silver
Angel-hair

1 Center candle, and add rosehips (**a**) and (**b**) extending toward both sides.

2 Hide *kenzan* with Angel-hair, forming a dome shape.

3 Place holly all around, adding more to front, back and middle left.

4 Add silver holly all around, adding more to front and right.

5 Finish with poinsettia slanting low from right end of container.

Gold Arrangement
(Left)

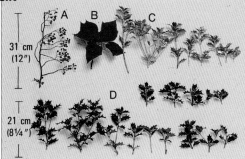

A   B   C
31 cm
(12″)
D
21 cm
(8¼″)

Materials: Rosehip (**A**)
Poinsettia (**B**)
Holly in gold (**C**)
Holly (**D**)
Others: *Kenzan* (needlepoint holder)
Candle in gold
Angel-hair

1 Center candle and add rosehips to left side almost horizontally.

73 on page 54

Materials:
Myriocladus (**A**)
Peach blossom (silk flower, **B**)
Dalta maidenhair fern (**C**)
Butterfly ornament (**D**)
Others:
Kenzan
(needlepoint holder)
Florist's foam

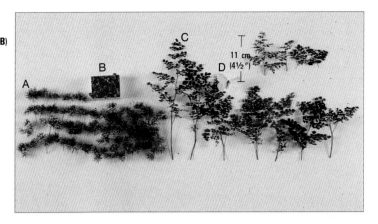

Container:

Diam 16 cm × H 8 cm (6½" × 3⅛")

Florist's foam shaped into a ball, 7 cm (2¾") in diameter. Soak in deep water 30 minutes.

1 Push myriocladus sprigs into florist's foam until it is completely covered.

2 Thrust a 40 cm (15½") twig into center of florist's foam.

3 Intersperse with silk flowers all around. Trim myriocladus to form a ball.

4 Cut end of twig at a slant and fix into center of *kenzan*. Insert maidenhair fern in a wind-blown shape.

5 Place maidenhair fern at base, spreading widely. Finish off with butterfly ornament.

2 Hide *kenzan* with Angel-hair, forming a dome shape.

3 Place fresh holly in front of Angel-hair, filling up to rim of container.

4 Add gold holly as appropriate, thickening at front right.

5 Finish with poinsettia behind Angel-hair slanting toward back right.

85 on page 63

Materials: Rose (**A**)
(red, **a**)
(custard, **b**)
Miniature rose (**B**)
(pink, **c**)
(yellow, **d**)

Container:

Diam 10 cm × H 27 cm (4" × 10½")

To keep roses fresh longer, drain the stem ends and burn over the flame of a gas burner or alcohol lamp and dip into cold water immediately.

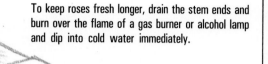

Protect blossoms and leaves with wet newspaper.

1 Place roses (**a**) of various lengths so they extend almost horizontally, toward right but not hanging below rim of vase.

2 Place roses (**b**) to middle to left of container, forming a dome shape.

3 Insert miniature roses (**c**) between (**a**) and (**b**), thicker toward left.

4 Insert (**d**) at front, middle and back for finished arrangement.

5 Rear view of finished arrangement.

6 Right-side view of finished arrangement. Notice whole arrangement is facing forward.

7 Left-side view of finished arrangement.

87 on page 65

Materials: Oriental hybrid lily (**A**), Rosy lily (**B**), Baby's breath (**C**), Weeping golden bell (**D**), Spirea (**F**)
Others: 2 *kenzan* (needlepoint holder)

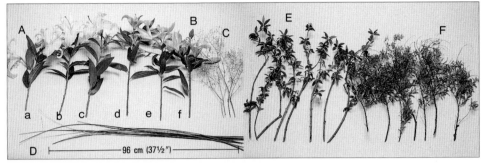

Container:

W 27 cm × D 10 cm × H 16 cm
(10½" × 4" × 6½")

1 Using 1/3 of container, stand a stem of weeping golden bell, then add more slanting toward front left.

2 Center a stem of weeping golden bell vertically, then add more to right side at a slant.

3 Place spirea sprigs to hide rim of container. Fan them out.

4 Center showly lily (**c**) slanting slightly toward your left shoulder.

5 Place (**A**) and (**b**) slanting toward your right shoulder.

6 Add rosy lilies (**d**), (**e**), (**f**) to middle, front left and back of arrangement.

7 Insert baby's breath in front, and bear-grass cascading from middle to right of arrangement.

8 Rear view of finished arrangement.

9 Right-side view of finished arrangement.

10 Left-side view of finished arrangement.

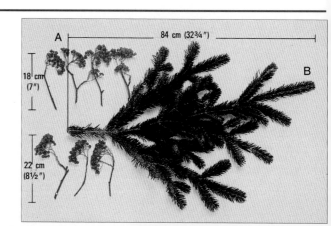

Container:

Materials: Mountain ash berry (**A**)
Fir (**B**)
Others: 8 pcs 35 cm (13½") 2.5 cm (1") ribbon in gold
4 pcs 35 cm (13½") 2.5 cm (1") ribbon in white
17 small bells
Kenzan (needlepoint holder)
Small vessel
#30 wire

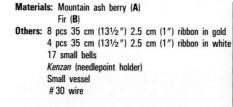

Diam 25 cm × H 66 cm
(9¾" × 25¾")

1 Position fir branch at center, slanting boldly toward your left shoulder.

2 Attach small bells and bows onto fir branch in a good proportion.

3 Fill out mouth of container with mountain ash berries forming a dome shape.

Ribbon

35 cm
(13¾")

8 pieces

2.5 cm
(1")

35 cm
(13¾")

2.5 cm
(1")

Tie around branch and make a bow.

Secure bells using wire.

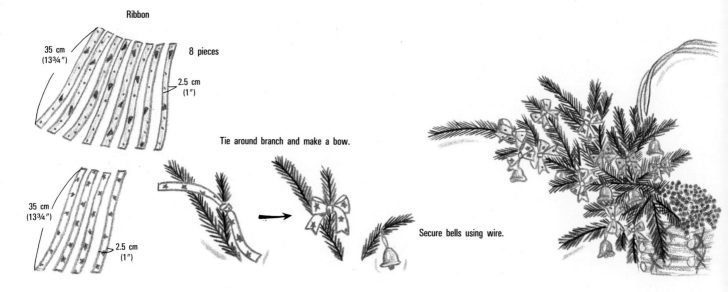

ARRANGEMENT ON BACK COVER

Materials: Solanum mammosum (**A**)
Dwarf sunflower (**B**)
Miniature rose (**C**)

Finished size: W 55 cm × H 17 cm (21½″ × 6¾″)

Container: W 9.5 cm × D 6.5 cm (3¾″ × 2½″)

1 Center solanum mammosum (**b**) slanting slightly forward.

2 Add (**a**) and (**c**) to both sides, at a slant.

3 Notice interval between (**b**) and (**c**) is wider than (**a**) and (**b**).

4 Place dwarf sunflower at left of (**b**), slanting toward your right shoulder.

5 Place another dwarf sunflower at right of (**b**) at a slant.

6 Place remaining dwarf sunflowers in front right, forming a triangle with flower heads.

7 Finish off by adding miniature roses low, near rim of container.

8 Rear view of finished arrangement.

9 Right-side view of finished arrangement. Check to see the directions of solanum mammosum and dwarf sunflowers.

CHOOSING MATERIALS

Although there are no rules or taboos when choosing floral materials, it seems that some combinations are more harmonious than others. For beginners of ikebana, a combination of branches and flowers is highly recommended. The strength of branches affects and complements the fragile beauty of flowers and creates a surprising effect which could never be achieved if either of them were used alone. In fact, there are some arranging styles using a single kind of foliage or flower, but a considerable amount of practice is essential to bend the materials. Therefore it is not appropriate for the beginner.

CUTTING MATERIALS

Cut away any leaves and branches that are damaged, broken, or too dense to define the stem lines clearly. If necessary, straighten a curved stem or bend a straight stem before cutting to the required length.

●Cutting a flower stem

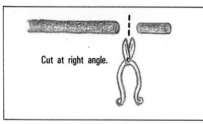

Cut at right angle.

Cut flowers quickly at right angle. Thin stems can be cut between points of scissors whereas thicker stems can be easily cut well inside the blades of the scissors. When cutting a hollow stalk such as calla lily, catch the stalk between the blades of the scissors, and rotate the stalk as you cut. Always remember that too much pressure on blades will crush the tissues of the stem.

●Cutting a branch

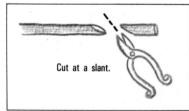

Cut at a slant.

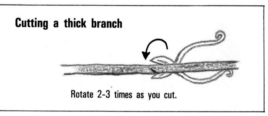

Cutting a thick branch

Rotate 2-3 times as you cut.

Cut branches diagonally so that the edges can be easily inserted into *kenzan* or pushed against the inner wall of the vase. Open the scissor handles wide, put the branch well inside the blades at an angle, and cut.

When the branch is too thick to cut with a single motion of the scissors, catch it well inside the blades and cut as far as you can. Remove scissors and repeat the same motion until completely cut. Another way of cutting a thick branch is rotating it as you cut the outside, then breaking it with both hands. A saw can be also used to cut very thick branches.

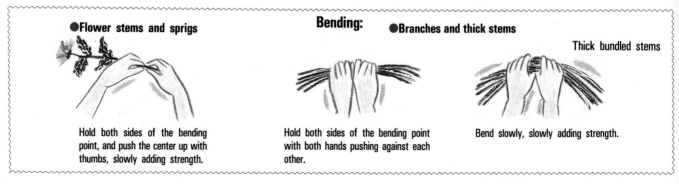

Bending:

●Flower stems and sprigs

Hold both sides of the bending point, and push the center up with thumbs, slowly adding strength.

●Branches and thick stems

Hold both sides of the bending point with both hands pushing against each other.

Thick bundled stems

Bend slowly, slowly adding strength.

CONDITIONING MATERIALS

Flowers tend to wilt prematurely if cut and exposed to the air. There are several traditional devices to help the stem ends absorb water easily. Before giving any special treatment, it is essential to cut the stems deep under water.

1. Cutting under Water

This is the basic preservation method to increase water intake. Cut the stems deep under water and the pressure allows the water to be drawn up easily. Every flower must be cut this way before being treated in any of the following methods.

Good for:
All except lotus and other water plants

2. Hot Water Treatment

Some flowers such as peony or amaranth tend to wither easily. Dip cut ends of flowers into hot water 1–2 minutes and then into cold water immediately. The difference of temperatures hastens water absorption. Baby's breath lasts longer with this treatment in winter.

Good for:
Globe amaranth
Patrinia scabiosafolia
Lady's mantle
Hollyhock
Amaranth

3. Charring

Wrap the blossoms and leaves in wet newspaper and char the cut ends over fire. Burn until the ends glow red for 1–2 minutes, then dip into cold water immediately.

Good for:
Rose, Miniature rose, Spray mum, Croton, Poinsettia, Satsuma mock orangre, Peony

4. Crushing

Hard, fibrous stems can be conditioned in this method. Using a side of closed scissors, crush the ends about 5 cm (2″). Thinner stems such as clematis can be crushed between your teeth. Leave the stems in water before arranging. If using *kenzan*: cut some of the crushed end.

Good for:
Spirea
Balloonflower

5. Breaking

Hard and fibrous flowers such as chrysanthemum can be just broken under water. This enlarges the surface area of the stem end and speeds water intake.

Good for:
Chrysanthemum, Small chrysanthemum, Spray mum

6. Splitting

Holding the branch with your hand diagonal cut end up, make a cross cut quickly. This method also enlarges the surface area of the stem end and speeds water intake.

Good for:
Japanese maholia
Camellia
Flowering quince
Maple

Chemical Treatments

Wipe dry the cut edges of material before applying the chemicals. This way the chemicals will be absorbed quickly.

7. Mint oil

This is used to disinfect the cut edges. Dip the end into mint oil before arranging in the container. The stem end of clematis should be crushed with a hammer or scissors before dipping.

Good for:
Caladium, Mountian laurel, Blazing-star
Clematis

8. Vinegar

Vinegar is used for its sterlizing effect on plants. Cut the stem end and immediately dip into vinegar before arranging.

Good for:
Bamboo, Japanese pampas, Shepherd's purse, Foxtail, Hordeum murimum, Begonia, Aster

9. Alcohol

Sake or whiskey is added to the water in the container after arranging.

Good for:
Smokegrass, Wisteria, Blazing-star

10. Burnt alum

If the stem is spongy, burnt alum is used to stimulate the cut surface to allow water to be absorbed easily. Rub burnt alum into the cut end.

Good for:
Hydrangea, Hydrangea macrophylla normalis, Cineraria

11. Salt

Salt is especially effective for flowers in bloom from summer to autumn. The stem end should be crushed before being rubbed with salt.

Good for:
Balloonflower, Sunflower, Great burnet, Caladium, Bird's nest fern

12. Plant food

Flowers which have a short life span, such as a few days, will last a week by adding plant food sold at florists.

Good for:
All flowers and foliage

FIXING MATERIALS
Securing the materials greatly differs depending on the arranging styles, i.e., *moribana and nageire*.

Moribana: Fixing onto *kenzan*

●Thin stems

Push the stem end into the spikes. Push until the cut end rests on the bottom of *kenzan*. Slant the stem, if necessary, after this securing procedure. If slanting low, push the end onto the spikes with enough strength to secure the side of the stem. The following are the techniques of fixing according to the pliability and thickness of the stems:

Capping

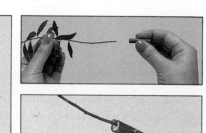

1 If the stem is sturdy but too thin to be secured on *kenzan*, it is often reinforced by capping with a thicker stem.

2 Cut 2 cm-3 cm (¾"-1⅛") long piece from a thicker stem, and insert the thin stem into this supporting cap.

| **Binding** | **Reinforcing A** | **Reinforcing B** | **Folding stems** | **Supporting** |

2cm
(¾")

A   B

Very thin stems can be bound together using wire to add thickness.

Stems with heavy heads or fragile stems are bound together with a short branch using wire.

Very thin stems can be wrapped with paper to add thickness.

If the stem is too thin to be secured in *kenzan*, bend the end to form a "V".

A: When slanting fragile stems, push a small piece of branch horizontally into *kenzan*, then place the material against it.

B: Stand a small piece of branch on *kenzan*, and rest the stem on it.

●Branches

Try to push branches into the spaces between the spikes rather than into the spikes themselves. (Cut the stem so the edge is slightly wider than the interval between the spikes.)

When slanting the stem, cut the edge at a slant so the balk remains on the slanting side. Push the stem upright into *kenzan*, and carefully slant it toward the longer side. Be sure the side of remaining balm is secured on *kenzan*.

Nageire: **Arranging without** *kenzan*

●**Cross-bar fixture** (fixed in vase):

From a strong and flexible branch, cut two pieces slightly longer than the diameter of the vase.

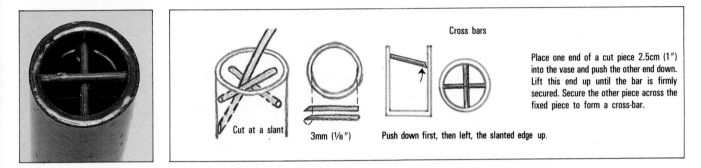

Cross bars

Place one end of a cut piece 2.5cm (1″) into the vase and push the other end down. Lift this end up until the bar is firmly secured. Secure the other piece across the fixed piece to form a cross-bar.

Cut at a slant   3mm (⅛″)   Push down first, then left, the slanted edge up.

●**Vertical bar fixture** (fixed on material):

When the branch has a heavy head and does not stay at a desired angle, a slit stalk is used to support it in place. Cut a piece of branch slightly shorter than the diameter of the vase. Split the end deep enough to hold the materials at the desired height. Split the end of the material and interlock with the supporting stalk in the vase. This way the material is secured at three points: the rim of the vase (**a**), interlocking point (**b**), and the inside wall of the vase (**c**). (If the material is too thin to split, thrust it into the slit.)

1 Cut the supporting stalk a little shorter than the height of the vase. Slit the end to the determined length.

2 Split the end slightly deeper than the interlocking point.

3 Interlock the slit material and the supporting stalk.

4 Adjust the angle of the cutting edge so it touches the inside wall of the vase.

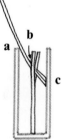

●**Direct fixing**

The branch rests only on two points of the vase: the rim and the inside wall of the vase.

Techniques for direct fixing

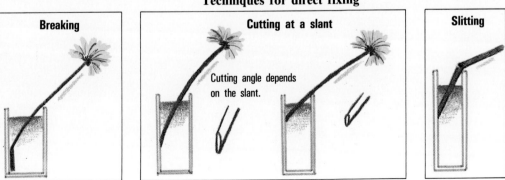

Breaking

Cutting at a slant

Cutting angle depends on the slant.

Slitting

Bending

IKEBANA UTENSILS

Scissors:

There are a few kinds of scissors or shears specially made for ikebana. Choose whichever is easy for you to handle. When cutting a branch, place the cutting point between the blades of scissors as deep as possible, and grasp firmly. Thicker branches can be easily cut by slitting the side of the cutting point. Rub oil on your scissors after every use to prevent from rusting.

Handling scissors:

1 Hold the upper handle between your thumb and palm, the lower handle with your fingers.

2 Hold tightly, without putting any finger between the handles.

Kenzan

Kenzan, or needlepoint holders for *moribana*, come in various shapes and sizes. They can hold the materials at any angle and they can be rearranged many times. Choose a heavy one with lots of spikes.

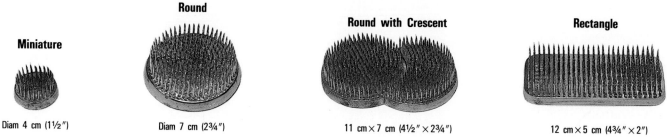

Miniature

Diam 4 cm (1½″)

Round

Diam 7 cm (2¾″)

Round with Crescent

11 cm × 7 cm (4½″ × 2¾″)

Rectangle

12 cm × 5 cm (4¾″ × 2″)

★ Sizes of *kenzan* are all standard.

Kenzan repairer:

Thick branches could easily bend the *kenzan* spikes. In this case, a needle repairer is used to straighten the spikes.

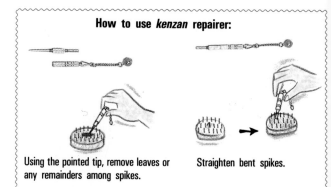

How to use *kenzan* repairer:

Using the pointed tip, remove leaves or any remainders among spikes.

Straighten bent spikes.

BASICS & TECHNIQUES OF IKEBANA

Saws:
A small folding saw is convenient when cutting thick branches or roots.

Wire:
Thin wire can be used to bind materials together.

Water spray:
For a floral display placed in a dry area or in an air-conditioned room, it is essential to give moisture occasionally. Spray water over the finished arrangement. It will also wash off any dirt or dust on leaves.

Bowl:
A deep bowl is used to cut materials under water to keep them fresh longer.

Chicken net:
Rolled chicken net can easily hold numbers of thick stems such as gladiolus or stock.

Pebbles:
Varieties of pebbles and marbles are used to hide and to give weight to *kenzan*. Choose pebbles that match the color of flowers.

Florist's foam:
This is usually sold in a block. Cut out a desired shape and soak in water. Be sure to give water frequently when displaying the arrangement for a long time.

BASICS & TECHNIQUES OF IKEBANA

IKEBANA CONTAINERS

Ikebana is never complete without an appropriate container. Consider the shape, color, size and texture of the container to match the floral materials.

Suiban (shallow container)

There are various shapes such as round, oval, rectangular, or triangular. One that has a 30 cm (11¾″) diameter and a 4 cm-5 cm (1½″ -2″) height is most recommended.

Tall Vase

The most practical vase would be about 30 cm–40 cm (11¾″–15½″) high, and 10 cm–15 cm (4″–5¾″) wide cylinder or prism type.

Compote

Compote shaped container is used specially for a modern arrangement or when a certain height is required for *moribana* arrangements.

Pot

Choose a heavy, stable pot with a small opening. When arranging, turn the pot around and check the best side to match the floral materials.

Bowl

Look around your house and find a possible container to match the arrangement.

Glass Vase

Clarity and a refreshing mood, the characteristics of glass ware create its own mood not only for summer but for any season and any style: traditional or modern. Showing the water is another feature of this kind of container, but pay special attention to the stems in the water of the vase.

Basket or Colander

Bamboo-woven baskets and colanders match well with floral materials because both are made of plants. Arrangements in woven containers create a warm and generous impression. Natural bamboo colander complements wild flowers picked in the field or in your garden. Be sure the water container is stable in the basket.

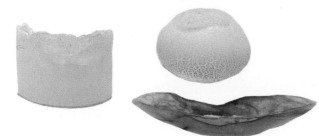

INDEX OF FLOWERS

Note: Page numbers in *italics* indicate instructions.